SHSAT MATH FOR BEGINNERS

The Ultimate Step by Step Guide to Preparing for the SHSAT Math Test

By

Reza Nazari

About Effortless Math Education

Effortless Math Education operates the www.effortlessmath.com website, which prepares and publishes Test prep and Mathematics learning resources. Effortless Math authors' team strives to prepare and publish the best quality Mathematics learning resources to make learning Math easier for all. We Help Students Learn to Love Mathematics.

All inquiries should be addressed to:
info@effortlessMath.com
www.EffortlessMath.com

ISBN: 978-1-64612-248-6

Published by: **Effortless Math Education Inc**

for Online Math Practice Visit www.EffortlessMath.com

Welcome to
SHSAT Math Prep
2022

Thank you for choosing Effortless Math for your SHSAT Math test preparation and congratulations on making the decision to take the SHSAT test! It's a remarkable move you are taking, one that shouldn't be diminished in any capacity. That's why you need to use every tool possible to ensure you succeed on the test with the highest possible score, and this extensive study guide is one such tool.

If math has never been a strong subject for you, **don't worry**! This book will help you prepare for (and even ACE) the SHSAT test's math section. As test day draws nearer, effective preparation becomes increasingly more important. Thankfully, you have this comprehensive study guide to help you get ready for the test. With this guide, you can feel confident that you will be more than ready for the SHSAT Math test when the time comes.

First and foremost, it is important to note that this book is a study guide and not a textbook. It is best read from cover to cover. Every lesson of this "self-guided math book" was carefully developed to ensure that you are making the most effective use of your time while preparing for the test. This up-to-date guide reflects the 2022 test guidelines and will put you on the right track to hone your math skills, overcome exam anxiety, and boost your confidence, so that you can have your best to succeed on the SHSAT Math test.

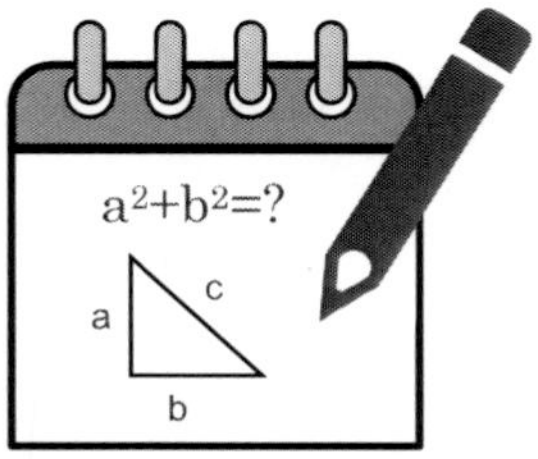

This study guide will:

☑ Explain the format of the SHSAT Math test.

☑ Describe specific test-taking strategies that you can use on the test.

☑ Provide SHSAT Math test-taking tips.

☑ Review all SHSAT Math concepts and topics you will be tested on.

☑ Help you identify the areas in which you need to concentrate your study time.

☑ Offer exercises that help you develop the basic math skills you will learn in each section.

☑ Give **2 realistic and full-length practice tests** (featuring new question types) with detailed answers to help you measure your exam readiness and build confidence.

This resource contains everything you will ever need to succeed on the SHSAT Math test. You'll get in-depth instructions on every math topic as well as tips and techniques on how to answer each question type. You'll also get plenty of practice questions to boost your test-taking confidence.

In addition, in the following pages you'll find:

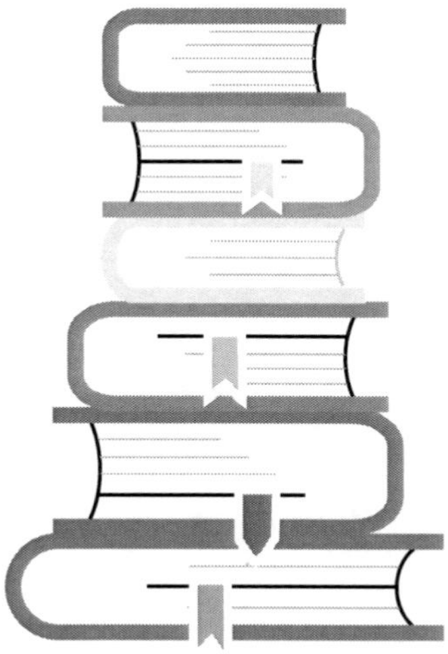

- **How to Use This Book Effectively** – This section provides you with step-by-step instructions on how to get the most out of this comprehensive study guide.
- **How to study for the SHSAT Math Test** – A six-step study program has been developed to help you make the best use of this book and prepare for your SHSAT Math test. Here you'll find tips and strategies

to guide your study program and help you understand SHSAT Math and how to ace the test.

- **SHSAT Math Review** – Learn everything you need to know about the SHSAT Math test.
- **SHSAT Math Test-Taking Strategies** – Learn how to effectively put these recommended test-taking techniques into use for improving your SHSAT Math score.
- **Test Day Tips** – Review these tips to make sure you will do your best when the big day comes.

Effortless Math's SHSAT Online Center

Effortless Math Online SHSAT Center offers a complete study program, including the following:

- ✓ Step-by-step instructions on how to prepare for the SHSAT Math test
- ✓ Numerous SHSAT Math worksheets to help you measure your math skills
- ✓ Complete list of SHSAT Math formulas
- ✓ Video lessons for all SHSAT Math topics
- ✓ Full-length SHSAT Math practice tests
- ✓ And much more...

No Registration Required.

Visit effortlessmath.com/SHSAT to find your online SHSAT Math resources.

How to Use This Book Effectively

Look no further when you need a study guide to improve your math skills to succeed on the math portion of the SHSAT test. Each chapter of this comprehensive guide to the SHSAT Math will provide you with the knowledge, tools, and understanding needed for every topic covered on the test.

It's imperative that you understand each topic before moving onto another one, as that's the way to guarantee your success. Each topic provides you with examples and a step-by-step guide of every concept to better understand the content that will be on the test. To get the best possible results from this book:

- **Begin studying long before your test date**. This provides you ample time to learn the different math concepts. The earlier you begin studying for the test, the sharper your skills will be. Do not procrastinate! Provide yourself with plenty of time to learn the concepts and feel comfortable that you understand them when your test date arrives.
- **Practice consistently**. Study SHSAT Math concepts at least 20 to 30 minutes a day. Remember, slow and steady wins the race, which can be applied to preparing for the SHSAT Math test. Instead of cramming to tackle everything at once, be patient and learn the math topics in short bursts.
- Whenever you get a math problem wrong, **mark it off, and review it later** to make sure you understand the concept.
- Start each session by **looking over the previous material.**
- Once you've reviewed the book's lessons, **take the practice test at the back of the book** to gauge your level of readiness. Then, review your results. Read detailed answers and solutions for each question you missed.
- **Take another practice test** to get an idea of how ready you are to take the actual exam. Taking the practice tests will give you the confidence you need on test day. Simulate the SHSAT testing environment by sitting in a quiet room free from distraction. Make sure to clock yourself with a timer.

How to Study for the SHSAT Math Test

Studying for the SHSAT Math test can be a really daunting and boring task. What's the best way to go about it? Is there a certain study method that works better than others? Well, studying for the SHSAT Math can be done effectively. The following six-step program has been designed to make preparing for the SHSAT Math test more efficient and less overwhelming.

Step **1** - Create a study plan
Step **2** - Choose your study resources
Step **3** - Review, Learn, Practice
Step **4** - Learn and practice test-taking strategies
Step **5** - Learn the SHSAT Test format and take practice tests
Step **6** - Analyze your performance

STEP 1: Create a Study Plan

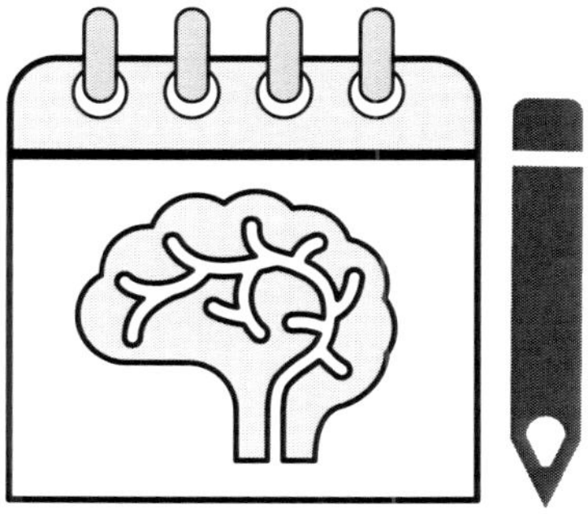

It's always easier to get things done when you have a plan. Creating a study plan for the SHSAT Math test can help you to stay on track with your studies. It's important to sit down and prepare a study plan with what works with your life, work, and any other obligations you may have. Devote enough time each day to studying. It's also a great idea to break down each section of the exam into blocks and study one concept at a time.
It's important to understand that there is no "right" way to create a study plan. Your study plan will be personalized based on your specific needs and learning style.
Follow these guidelines to create an effective study plan for your SHSAT Math test:

★ **Analyze your learning style and study habits** – Everyone has a different learning style. It is essential to embrace your individuality and the unique way you learn. Think about what works and what doesn't work for you. Do you prefer SHSAT Math prep books or a combination of textbooks and video lessons? Does it work better for you if you study every night for thirty minutes or is it more effective to study in the morning before going to work?

★ **Evaluate your schedule** – Review your current schedule and find out how much time you can consistently devote to SHSAT Math study.

★ **Develop a schedule** – Now it's time to add your study schedule to your calendar like any other obligation. Schedule time for study, practice, and review. Plan out which topic you will study on which day to ensure that you're devoting enough time to each concept. Develop a study plan that is mindful, realistic, and flexible.

★ **Stick to your schedule** – A study plan is only effective when it is followed consistently. You should try to develop a study plan that you can follow for the length of your study program.

★ **Evaluate your study plan and adjust as needed** – Sometimes you need to adjust your plan when you have new commitments. Check in with yourself regularly to make sure that you're not falling behind in your study plan. Remember, the most important thing is sticking to your plan. Your study plan is all about helping you be more productive. If you find that your study plan is not as effective as you want, don't get discouraged. It's okay to make changes as you figure out what works best for you.

Step 2: Choose Your Study Resources

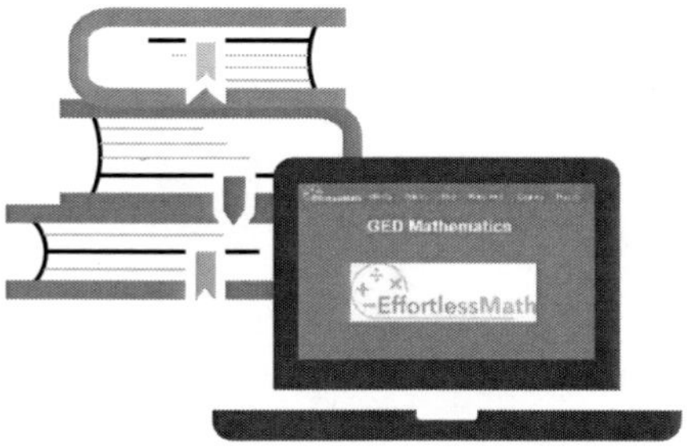

There are numerous textbooks and online resources available for the SHSAT Math test, and it may not be clear where to begin. Don't worry! This study guide provides everything you need to fully prepare for your SHSAT Math test. In addition to the book content, you can also use Effortless Math's online resources. (video lessons, worksheets, formulas, etc.)

On each page, there is a link (and a QR code) to an online webpage which provides a comprehensive review of the topic, step-by-step instruction, video tutorial, and numerous examples and exercises to help you fully understand the concept.

Simply visit EffortlessMath.com/SHSAT to find your online SHSAT Math resources.

Step 3: Review, Learn, Practice

This SHSAT Math study guide breaks down each subject into specific skills or content areas. For instance, the percent concept is separated into different topics–percent calculation, percent increase and decrease, percent problems, etc. Use this book to help you go over all key math concepts and topics on the SHSAT Math test.

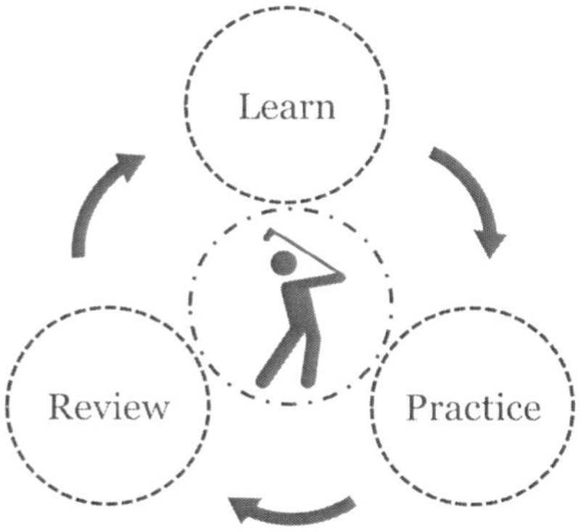

As you read each chapter, take notes or highlight the concepts you would like to go over again in the future. If you're unfamiliar with a topic or something is difficult for you, do additional research on it. For each math topic, plenty of instructions, step-by-step guides, and examples are provided to ensure you get a good grasp of the material. You can also find video lessons on the Effortless Math website for each SHSAT Math concept.

Quickly review the topics you do understand to get a brush-up of the material. Be sure to do the practice questions provided at the end of every chapter to measure your understanding of the concepts.

Step 4: Learn and Practice Test-taking Strategies

In the following sections, you will find important test-taking strategies and tips that can help you earn extra points. You'll learn how to think strategically and when to guess if you don't know the answer to a question. Using SHSAT Math test-taking strategies and tips can help you raise your score and do well on the test. Apply test taking strategies on the practice tests to help you boost your confidence.

Step 5: Learn the SHSAT Test Format and Take Practice Tests

The SHSAT *Test Review* section provides information about the structure of the SHSAT test. Read this section to learn more about the SHSAT test structure, different test sections, the number of questions in each section, and the section time limits. When you have a prior understanding of the test format and different types of SHSAT Math questions, you'll feel more confident when you take the actual exam.

Once you have read through the instructions and lessons and feel like you are ready to go – take advantage of both of the full-length SHSAT Math practice tests available in this study guide. Use the practice tests to sharpen your skills and build confidence.

The SHSAT Math practice tests offered at the end of the book are formatted similarly to the actual SHSAT Math test. When you take each practice test, try to simulate actual testing conditions. To take the practice tests, sit in a quiet space, time yourself, and work through as many of the questions as time allows.

The practice tests are followed by detailed answer explanations to help you find your weak areas, learn from your mistakes, and raise your SHSAT Math score.

STEP 6: Analyze Your Performance

After taking the practice tests, look over the answer keys and explanations to learn which questions you answered correctly and which you did not. Never be discouraged if you make a few mistakes. See them as a learning opportunity. This will highlight your strengths and weaknesses.

You can use the results to determine if you need additional practice or if you are ready to take the actual SHSAT Math test.

Looking for more?

Visit effortlessmath.com/SHSAT to find hundreds of SHSAT Math worksheets, video tutorials, practice tests, SHSAT Math formulas, and much more.

Or scan this QR code.

No Registration Required.

SHSAT Test Review

The Specialized High School Admissions Test, commonly known as the SHSAT, is a standardized test that is administered by the New York City Department of Education. SHSAT is the criterion for admissions to New York City Specialized High Schools. It is available to 8th grade students in New York City. 9th grade students may also choose to take the 9th grade version of the SHSAT.

The SHSAT assesses English Comprehension (Verbal) and Mathematics knowledge and skills.

The Mathematics section of the test is a 75-minute test that covers basic mathematics topics, quantitative problem-solving and algebraic questions. There are 5 Gridded-Response and 52 multiple choice questions in the Math section of SHSAT and students have 75 minutes to complete this section. Calculator is NOT allowed for the SHSAT test.

In this book, we have covered all Mathematics topics students need to know. Now, it's time to take a real SHSAT Math test. In this section, there are two complete SHSAT Mathematics Tests. Take these tests to see what score you'll be able to receive on a real SHSAT test.

SHSAT Math Test-Taking Strategies

Here are some test-taking strategies that you can use to maximize your performance and results on the SHSAT Math test.

#1 : Use This Approach To Answer Every SHSAT Math Question

- Review the question to identify keywords and important information.
- Translate the keywords into math operations so you can solve the problem.
- Review the answer choices. What are the differences between answer choices?
- Draw or label a diagram if needed.
- Try to find patterns.
- Find the right method to answer the question. Use straightforward math, plug in numbers, or test the answer choices (backsolving).
- Double-check your work.

#2 : Use Educated Guessing

This approach is applicable to the problems you understand to some degree but cannot solve using straightforward math. In such cases, try to filter out as many answer choices as possible before picking an answer. In cases where you don't have a clue about what a certain problem entails, don't waste any time trying to eliminate answer choices. Just choose one randomly before moving onto the next question.

As you can ascertain, direct solutions are the most optimal approach. Carefully read through the question, determine what the solution is using the math you have learned before, then coordinate the answer with one of the choices available to you. Are you stumped? Make your best guess, then move on. Don't leave any fields empty! Even if you're unable to work out a problem, strive to answer it. Take a guess if you have to. You will not lose points by getting an answer wrong, though you may gain a point by getting it correct!

#3: Ballpark

A ballpark answer is a rough approximation. When we become overwhelmed by calculations and figures, we end up making silly mistakes. A decimal that is moved by one unit can change an answer from right to wrong, regardless of the number of steps that you went through to get it. That's where ballparking can play a big part.

If you think you know what the correct answer may be (even if it's just a ballpark answer), you'll usually have the ability to eliminate a couple of choices. While answer choices are usually based on the average student error and/or values that are closely tied, you will still be able to weed out choices that are way far afield. Try to find answers that aren't in the proverbial ballpark when you're looking for a wrong answer on a multiple-choice question. This is an optimal approach to eliminating answers to a problem.

#4: Backsolving

A majority of questions on the SHSAT Math test will be in multiple-choice format. Many test-takers prefer multiple-choice questions, as at least the answer is right there. You'll typically have four answers to pick from. You simply need to figure out which one is correct. Usually, the best way to go about doing so is "backsolving."

As mentioned earlier, direct solutions are the most optimal approach to answering a question. Carefully read through a problem, calculate a solution, then correspond the answer with one of the choices displayed in front of you. If you can't calculate a solution, your next best approach involves "backsolving."

When backsolving a problem, contrast one of your answer options against the problem you are asked, then see which of them is most relevant. More often than not, answer choices are listed in ascending or descending order. In such cases, try out the choices B or C. If it's not correct, you can go either down or up from there.

#5 : Plugging In Numbers

"Plugging in numbers" is a strategy that can be applied to a wide range of different math problems on the SHSAT Math test. This approach is typically used to simplify a challenging question so that it is more understandable. By using the strategy carefully, you can find the answer without too much trouble.

The concept is fairly straightforward–replace unknown variables in a problem with certain values. When selecting a number, consider the following:

- Choose a number that's basic (just not too basic). Generally, you should avoid choosing 1 (or even 0). A decent choice is 2.
- Try not to choose a number that is displayed in the problem.
- Make sure you keep your numbers different if you need to choose at least two of them.
- More often than not, choosing numbers merely lets you filter out some of your answer choices. As such, don't just go with the first choice that gives you the right answer.
- If several answers seem correct, then you'll need to choose another value and try again. This time, though, you'll just need to check choices that haven't been eliminated yet.
- If your question contains fractions, then a potential right answer may involve either an LCD (least common denominator) or an LCD multiple.
- 100 is the number you should choose when you are dealing with problems involving percentages.

SHSAT Math – Test Day Tips

After practicing and reviewing all the math concepts you've been taught, and taking some SHSAT mathematics practice tests, you'll be prepared for test day. Consider the following tips to be extra-ready come test time.

Before Your Test

What to do the night before:

- **Relax!** One day before your test, study lightly or skip studying altogether. You shouldn't attempt to learn something new, either. There are plenty of reasons why studying the evening before a big test can work against you. Put it this way–a marathoner wouldn't go out for a sprint before the day of a big race. Mental marathoners–such as yourself–should not study for any more than one hour 24 hours before a SHSAT test. That's because your brain requires some rest to be at its best. The night before your exam, spend some time with family or friends, or read a book.

- **Avoid bright screens** - You'll have to get some good shuteye the night before your test. Bright screens (such as the ones coming from your laptop, TV, or mobile device) should be avoided altogether. Staring at such a screen will keep your brain up, making it hard to drift asleep at a reasonable hour.

- **Make sure your dinner is healthy** - The meal that you have for dinner should be nutritious. Be sure to drink plenty of water as well. Load up on your complex carbohydrates, much like a marathon runner would do. Pasta, rice, and potatoes are ideal options here, as are vegetables and protein sources.

- **Get your bag ready for test day** - The night prior to your test, pack your bag with your stationery, admissions pass, ID, and any other gear that you need. Keep the bag right by your front door.

- **Make plans to reach the testing site** - Before going to sleep, ensure that you understand precisely how you will arrive at the site of the test. If parking is something you'll have to find first, plan for it. If you're dependent on public transit, then review the schedule. You should also make sure that the train/bus/subway/streetcar you use will be running. Find out about road closures as well. If a parent or friend is accompanying you, ensure that they understand what steps they have to take as well.

The Day of the Test

- **Get up reasonably early, but not too early.**
- **Have breakfast** - Breakfast improves your concentration, memory, and mood. As such, make sure the breakfast that you eat in the morning is healthy. The last thing you want to be is distracted by a grumbling tummy. If it's not your own stomach making those noises, another test taker close to you might be instead. Prevent discomfort or embarrassment by consuming a healthy breakfast. Bring a snack with you if you think you'll need it.
- **Follow your daily routine** - Do you watch Good Morning America each morning while getting ready for the day? Don't break your usual habits on the day of the test. Likewise, if coffee isn't something you drink in the morning, then don't take up the habit hours before your test. Routine consistency lets you concentrate on the main objective–doing the best you can on your test.
- **Wear layers** - Dress yourself up in comfortable layers. You should be ready for any kind of internal temperature. If it gets too warm during the test, take a layer off.
- **Get there on time** - The last thing you want to do is get to the test site late. Rather, you should be there 45 minutes prior to the start of the test. Upon your arrival, try not to hang out with anybody who is nervous. Any anxious energy they exhibit shouldn't influence you.
- **Leave the books at home** - No books should be brought to the test site. If you start developing anxiety before the test, books could encourage you to do some last-minute studying, which will only hinder you. Keep the books far away–better yet, leave them at home.

- **Make your voice heard** - If something is off, speak to a proctor. If medical attention is needed or if you'll require anything, consult the proctor prior to the start of the test. Any doubts you have should be clarified. You should be entering the test site with a state of mind that is completely clear.

- **Have faith in yourself** - When you feel confident, you will be able to perform at your best. When you are waiting for the test to begin, envision yourself receiving an outstanding result. Try to see yourself as someone who knows all the answers, no matter what the questions are. A lot of athletes tend to use this technique–particularly before a big competition. Your expectations will be reflected by your performance.

During your test

- **Be calm and breathe deeply** - You need to relax before the test, and some deep breathing will go a long way to help you do that. Be confident and calm. You got this. Everybody feels a little stressed out just before an evaluation of any kind is set to begin. Learn some effective breathing exercises. Spend a minute meditating before the test starts. Filter out any negative thoughts you have. Exhibit confidence when having such thoughts.

- **Concentrate on the test** - Refrain from comparing yourself to anyone else. You shouldn't be distracted by the people near you or random noise. Concentrate exclusively on the test. If you find yourself irritated by surrounding noises, earplugs can be used to block sounds off close to you. Don't forget–the test is going to last several hours if you're taking more than one subject of the test. Some of that time will be dedicated to brief sections. Concentrate on the specific section you are working on during a particular moment. Do not let your mind wander off to upcoming or previous sections.

- **Skip challenging questions** - Optimize your time when taking the test. Lingering on a single question for too long will work against you. If you don't know what the answer is to a certain question, use your best guess, and mark the question so you can review it later on. There is no need to spend time attempting to solve something you aren't sure about. That time would be better served handling the questions you can actually answer well. You will not be penalized for getting the wrong answer on a test like this.

- **Try to answer each question individually** - Focus only on the question you are working on. Use one of the test-taking strategies to solve the problem. If you aren't able to come up with an answer, don't get frustrated. Simply skip that question, then move onto the next one.

- **Don't forget to breathe!** Whenever you notice your mind wandering, your stress levels boosting, or frustration brewing, take a thirty-second break. Shut your eyes, drop your pencil, breathe deeply, and let your shoulders relax. You will end up being more productive when you allow yourself to relax for a moment.

- **Review your answer**. If you still have time at the end of the test, don't waste it. Go back and check over your answers. It is worth going through the test from start to finish to ensure that you didn't make a sloppy mistake somewhere.

- **Optimize your breaks** - When break time comes, use the restroom, have a snack, and reactivate your energy for the subsequent section. Doing some stretches can help stimulate your blood flow.

After your test

- **Take it easy** - You will need to set some time aside to relax and decompress once the test has concluded. There is no need to stress yourself out about what you could've said, or what you may have done wrong. At this point, there's nothing you can do about it. Your energy and time would be better spent on something that will bring you happiness for the remainder of your day.

- **Redoing the test** - Did you pass the test? Congratulations! Your hard work paid off! Passing this test means that you are now as knowledgeable as somebody who has graduated high school.

  If you have failed your test, though, don't worry! The test can be retaken. In such cases, you will need to follow the retake policy established by your state. You also need to re-register to take the exam again.

Contents

CHAPTER

1 Fractions and Mixed Numbers

Math topics that you'll learn in this chapter:

- ☑ Simplifying Fractions
- ☑ Adding and Subtracting Fractions
- ☑ Multiplying and Dividing Fractions
- ☑ Adding Mixed Numbers
- ☑ Subtracting Mixed Numbers
- ☑ Multiplying Mixed Numbers
- ☑ Dividing Mixed Numbers

Simplifying Fractions

- A fraction contains two numbers separated by a bar between them. The bottom number, called the denominator, is the total number of equally divided portions in one whole. The top number, called the numerator, is how many portions you have. And the bar represents the operation of division.
- Simplifying a fraction means reducing it to the lowest terms. To simplify a fraction, evenly divide both the top and bottom of the fraction by $2, 3, 5, 7$, etc.
- Continue until you can't go any further.

Examples:

Example 1. Simplify $\frac{18}{30}$

Solution: To simplify $\frac{18}{30}$, find a number that both 18 and 30 are divisible by. Both are divisible by 6. Then: $\frac{18}{30} = \frac{18 \div 6}{30 \div 6} = \frac{3}{5}$

Example 2. Simplify $\frac{32}{80}$

Solution: To simplify $\frac{32}{80}$, find a number that both 32 and 80 are divisible by. Both are divisible by 8 and 16. Then: $\frac{32}{80} = \frac{32 \div 8}{80 \div 8} = \frac{4}{10}$, 4 and 10 are divisible by 2, then: $\frac{4}{10} = \frac{2}{5}$ or $\frac{32}{80} = \frac{32 \div 16}{80 \div 16} = \frac{2}{5}$

Example 3. Simplify $\frac{40}{120}$

Solution: To simplify $\frac{40}{120}$, find a number that both 40 and 120 are divisible by. Both are divisible by 40, then: $\frac{40}{120} = \frac{40 \div 40}{120 \div 40} = \frac{1}{3}$

Adding and Subtracting Fractions

- For "like" fractions (fractions with the same denominator), add or subtract the numerators (top numbers) and write the answer over the common denominator (bottom numbers).
- Adding and Subtracting fractions with the same denominator:

$\frac{a}{b}+\frac{c}{b}=\frac{a+c}{b}$ $\qquad$ $\frac{a}{b}-\frac{c}{b}=\frac{a-c}{b}$

- Find equivalent fractions with the same denominator before you can add or subtract fractions with different denominators.
- Adding and Subtracting fractions with different denominators:

$$\frac{a}{b}+\frac{c}{d}=\frac{ad+bc}{bd} \qquad \frac{a}{b}-\frac{c}{d}=\frac{ad-bc}{bd}$$

Examples:

Example 1. Find the sum. $\frac{2}{3}+\frac{1}{2}=$

Solution: These two fractions are "unlike" fractions. (they have different denominators). Use this formula: $\frac{a}{b}+\frac{c}{d}=\frac{ad+cb}{bd}$

Then: $\frac{2}{3}+\frac{1}{2}=\frac{(2)(2)+(3)(1)}{3\times 2}=\frac{4+3}{6}=\frac{7}{6}$

Example 2. Find the difference. $\frac{3}{5}-\frac{2}{7}=$

Solution: For "unlike" fractions, find equivalent fractions with the same denominator before you can add or subtract fractions with different denominators. Use this formula: $\frac{a}{b}-\frac{c}{d}=\frac{ad-bc}{bd}$

$\frac{3}{5}-\frac{2}{7}=\frac{(3)(7)-(2)(5)}{5\times 7}=\frac{21-10}{35}=\frac{11}{35}$

Multiplying and Dividing Fractions

- **Multiplying fractions:** multiply the top numbers and multiply the bottom numbers. Simplify if necessary. $\frac{a}{b} \times \frac{c}{d} = \frac{a \times c}{b \times d}$
- **Dividing fractions:** Keep, Change, Flip
- Keep the first fraction, change the division sign to multiplication, and flip the numerator and denominator of the second fraction. Then, solve!

$$\frac{a}{b} \div \frac{c}{d} = \frac{a}{b} \times \frac{d}{c} = \frac{a \times d}{b \times c}$$

Examples:

Example 1. Multiply. $\frac{2}{3} \times \frac{3}{5} =$

Solution: Multiply the top numbers and multiply the bottom numbers.
$\frac{2}{3} \times \frac{3}{5} = \frac{2 \times 3}{3 \times 5} = \frac{6}{15}$, now, simplify: $\frac{6}{15} = \frac{6 \div 3}{15 \div 3} = \frac{2}{5}$

Example 2. Solve. $\frac{3}{4} \div \frac{2}{5} =$

Solution: Keep the first fraction, change the division sign to multiplication, and flip the numerator and denominator of the second fraction.
Then: $\frac{3}{4} \div \frac{2}{5} = \frac{3}{4} \times \frac{5}{2} = \frac{3 \times 5}{4 \times 2} = \frac{15}{8}$

Example 3. Calculate. $\frac{4}{5} \times \frac{3}{4} =$

Solution: Multiply the top numbers and multiply the bottom numbers.
$\frac{4}{5} \times \frac{3}{4} = \frac{4 \times 3}{5 \times 4} = \frac{12}{20}$, simplify: $\frac{12}{20} = \frac{12 \div 4}{20 \div 4} = \frac{3}{5}$

Example 4. Solve. $\frac{5}{6} \div \frac{3}{7} =$

Solution: Keep the first fraction, change the division sign to multiplication, and flip the numerator and denominator of the second fraction.
Then: $\frac{5}{6} \div \frac{3}{7} = \frac{5}{6} \times \frac{7}{3} = \frac{5 \times 7}{6 \times 3} = \frac{35}{18}$

Adding Mixed Numbers

Use the following steps for adding mixed numbers:

- Add whole numbers of the mixed numbers.
- Add the fractions of the mixed numbers.
- Find the Least Common Denominator (LCD) if necessary.
- Add whole numbers and fractions.
- Write your answer in lowest terms.

Examples:

Example 1. Add mixed numbers. $2\frac{1}{2}+1\frac{2}{3}=$

Solution: Let's rewriting our equation with parts separated, $2\frac{1}{2}+1\frac{2}{3}=2+\frac{1}{2}+1+\frac{2}{3}$.
Now, add whole number parts: $2+1=3$
Add the fraction parts $\frac{1}{2}+\frac{2}{3}$. Rewrite to solve with the equivalent fractions. $\frac{1}{2}+\frac{2}{3}=\frac{3}{6}+\frac{4}{6}=\frac{7}{6}$. The answer is an improper fraction (numerator is bigger than denominator). Convert the improper fraction into a mixed number: $\frac{7}{6}=1\frac{1}{6}$. Now, combine the whole and fraction parts: $3+1\frac{1}{6}=4\frac{1}{6}$

Example 2. Find the sum. $1\frac{3}{4}+2\frac{1}{2}=$

Solution: Rewriting our equation with parts separated, $1+\frac{3}{4}+2+\frac{1}{2}$. Add the whole number parts:
$1+2=3$. Add the fraction parts: $\frac{3}{4}+\frac{1}{2}=\frac{3}{4}+\frac{2}{4}=\frac{5}{4}$
Convert the improper fraction into a mixed number: $\frac{5}{4}=1\frac{1}{4}$.
Now, combine the whole and fraction parts: $3+1\frac{1}{4}=4\frac{1}{4}$

bit.ly/2M4oABB

Find more at

Subtracting Mixed Numbers

Use these steps for subtracting mixed numbers.

- Convert mixed numbers into improper fractions. $a\frac{c}{b}=\frac{ab+c}{b}$
- Find equivalent fractions with the same denominator for unlike fractions. (fractions with different denominators)
- Subtract the second fraction from the first one. $\frac{a}{b}-\frac{c}{d}=\frac{ad-bc}{bd}$
- Write your answer in lowest terms.
- If the answer is an improper fraction, convert it into a mixed number.

Examples:

Example 1. Subtract. $2\frac{1}{3}-1\frac{1}{2}=$

Solution: Convert mixed numbers into fractions: $2\frac{1}{3}=\frac{2\times3+1}{3}=\frac{7}{3}$ and $1\frac{1}{2}=\frac{1\times2+1}{2}=\frac{3}{2}$

These two fractions are "unlike" fractions. (they have different denominators). Find equivalent fractions with the same denominator. Use this formula: $\frac{a}{b}-\frac{c}{d}=\frac{ad-bc}{bd}$

$\frac{7}{3}-\frac{3}{2}=\frac{(7)(2)-(3)(3)}{3\times2}=\frac{14-9}{6}=\frac{5}{6}$

Example 2. Find the difference. $3\frac{4}{7}-2\frac{3}{4}=$

Solution: Convert mixed numbers into fractions: $3\frac{4}{7}=\frac{3\times7+4}{7}=\frac{25}{7}$ and $2\frac{3}{4}=\frac{2\times4+3}{4}=\frac{11}{4}$

Then: $3\frac{4}{7}-2\frac{3}{4}=\frac{25}{7}-\frac{11}{4}=\frac{(25)(4)-(11)(7)}{7\times4}=\frac{23}{28}$

Find more at bit.ly/3aD3KDG

Multiplying Mixed Numbers

Use the following steps for multiplying mixed numbers:

- Convert the mixed numbers into fractions. $a\frac{c}{b} = a + \frac{c}{b} = \frac{ab+c}{b}$
- Multiply fractions. $\frac{a}{b} \times \frac{c}{d} = \frac{a \times c}{b \times d}$
- Write your answer in lowest terms.
- If the answer is an improper fraction (numerator is bigger than denominator), convert it into a mixed number.

Examples:

Example 1. Multiply. $4\frac{1}{2} \times 2\frac{2}{5} =$

Solution: Convert mixed numbers into fractions, $4\frac{1}{2} = \frac{4\times2+1}{2} = \frac{9}{2}$ and $2\frac{2}{5} = \frac{2\times5+2}{5} = \frac{12}{5}$. Apply the fractions rule for multiplication: $\frac{9}{2} \times \frac{12}{5} = \frac{9\times12}{2\times5} = \frac{108}{10} = \frac{54}{5}$
The answer is an improper fraction. Convert it into a mixed number. $\frac{54}{5} = 10\frac{4}{5}$

Example 2. Multiply. $3\frac{2}{3} \times 2\frac{5}{6} =$

Solution: Converting mixed numbers into fractions, $3\frac{2}{3} \times 2\frac{5}{6} = \frac{11}{3} \times \frac{17}{6}$
Apply the fractions rule for multiplication: $\frac{11}{3} \times \frac{17}{6} = \frac{11\times17}{3\times6} = \frac{187}{18} = 10\frac{7}{18}$

Example 3. Find the product. $5\frac{1}{4} \times 3\frac{3}{8} =$

Solution: Convert mixed numbers to fractions: $5\frac{1}{4} = \frac{21}{4}$ and $3\frac{3}{8} = \frac{27}{8}$. Multiply two fractions:
$\frac{21}{4} \times \frac{27}{8} = \frac{21\times27}{4\times8} = \frac{567}{32} = 17\frac{23}{32}$

Dividing Mixed Numbers

Use the following steps for dividing mixed numbers:

- Convert the mixed numbers into fractions. $a\frac{c}{b} = a + \frac{c}{b} = \frac{ab + c}{b}$
- Divide fractions: Keep, Change, Flip: Keep the first fraction, change the division sign to multiplication, and flip the numerator and denominator of the second fraction. Then, solve! $\frac{a}{b} \div \frac{c}{d} = \frac{a}{b} \times \frac{d}{c} = \frac{a \times d}{b \times c}$
- Write your answer in lowest terms.
- If the answer is an improper fraction (numerator is bigger than denominator), convert it into a mixed number.

Examples:

Example 1. Solve. $2\frac{1}{3} \div 1\frac{1}{2}$

Solution: Convert mixed numbers into fractions: $2\frac{1}{3} = \frac{2\times3+1}{3} = \frac{7}{3}$ and $1\frac{1}{2} = \frac{1\times2+1}{2} = \frac{3}{2}$

Keep, Change, Flip: $\frac{7}{3} \div \frac{3}{2} = \frac{7}{3} \times \frac{2}{3} = \frac{7\times2}{3\times3} = \frac{14}{9}$. The answer is an improper fraction. Convert it into a mixed number: $\frac{14}{9} = 1\frac{5}{9}$

Example 2. Solve. $3\frac{3}{4} \div 2\frac{2}{5}$

Solution: Convert mixed numbers to fractions, then solve:

$3\frac{3}{4} \div 2\frac{2}{5} = \frac{15}{4} \div \frac{12}{5} = \frac{15}{4} \times \frac{5}{12} = \frac{75}{48} = 1\frac{9}{16}$

Example 3. Solve. $2\frac{4}{5} \div 1\frac{2}{3}$

Solution: Converting mixed numbers to fractions: $2\frac{4}{5} \div 1\frac{2}{3} = \frac{14}{5} \div \frac{5}{3}$

Keep, Change, Flip: $\frac{14}{5} \div \frac{5}{3} = \frac{14}{5} \times \frac{3}{5} = \frac{14\times3}{5\times5} = \frac{42}{25} = 1\frac{17}{25}$

Chapter 1: Practices

Simplify each fraction.

1) $\frac{2}{8} =$

2) $\frac{5}{15} =$

3) $\frac{10}{90} =$

4) $\frac{12}{16} =$

5) $\frac{25}{45} =$

6) $\frac{42}{54} =$

7) $\frac{48}{60} =$

8) $\frac{52}{169} =$

Find the sum or difference.

9) $\frac{3}{10} + \frac{2}{10} =$

10) $\frac{4}{9} - \frac{1}{9} =$

11) $\frac{2}{3} + \frac{6}{15} =$

12) $\frac{17}{24} - \frac{5}{8} =$

13) $\frac{7}{54} - \frac{1}{9} =$

14) $\frac{4}{5} - \frac{1}{6} =$

15) $\frac{6}{7} - \frac{3}{8} =$

16) $\frac{2}{13} + \frac{1}{4} =$

Find the products or quotients.

17) $\frac{2}{9} \div \frac{4}{3} =$

18) $\frac{14}{5} \div \frac{28}{35} =$

19) $\frac{9}{25} \times \frac{5}{27} =$

20) $\frac{65}{72} \times \frac{12}{15} =$

Find the sum.

21) $2\frac{1}{5} + 1\frac{2}{5} =$

22) $5\frac{1}{9} + 2\frac{7}{9} =$

23) $2\frac{3}{4} + 1\frac{1}{8} =$

24) $2\frac{2}{7} + 4\frac{1}{21} =$

25) $5\frac{3}{5} + 1\frac{4}{9} =$

26) $3\frac{3}{11} + 4\frac{6}{7} =$

Find the difference.

27) $5\frac{1}{3} - 4\frac{2}{3} =$

28) $4\frac{7}{10} - 1\frac{3}{10} =$

29) $3\frac{1}{3} - 2\frac{2}{9} =$

30) $6\frac{1}{2} - 3\frac{1}{3} =$

31) $4\frac{3}{4} - 2\frac{1}{28} =$

32) $4\frac{2}{7} - 3\frac{1}{6} =$

33) $5\frac{3}{10} - 3\frac{3}{4} =$

34) $6\frac{9}{20} - 2\frac{1}{3} =$

Find the products.

35) $1\frac{1}{2} \times 2\frac{3}{7} =$

36) $1\frac{3}{4} \times 1\frac{3}{5} =$

37) $4\frac{1}{2} \times 1\frac{5}{6} =$

38) $1\frac{2}{7} \times 3\frac{1}{5} =$

39) $2\frac{1}{5} \times 5\frac{1}{2} =$

40) $2\frac{1}{2} \times 4\frac{4}{5} =$

41) $3\frac{1}{5} \times 4\frac{1}{2} =$

42) $4\frac{9}{10} \times 4\frac{1}{2} =$

Solve.

43) $1\frac{1}{3} \div 1\frac{2}{3} =$

44) $2\frac{1}{4} \div 1\frac{1}{2} =$

45) $5\frac{1}{3} \div 3\frac{1}{2} =$

46) $3\frac{2}{7} \div 1\frac{1}{8} =$

47) $4\frac{1}{5} \div 2\frac{2}{3} =$

48) $1\frac{2}{3} \div 1\frac{3}{8} =$

49) $4\frac{1}{2} \div 2\frac{2}{3} =$

50) $1\frac{2}{11} \div 1\frac{1}{8} =$

Chapter 1: Answers

1) $\frac{1}{4}$
2) $\frac{1}{3}$
3) $\frac{1}{9}$
4) $\frac{3}{4}$
5) $\frac{5}{9}$
6) $\frac{7}{9}$
7) $\frac{4}{5}$
8) $\frac{4}{13}$
9) $\frac{1}{2}$
10) $\frac{1}{3}$
11) $\frac{16}{15} = 1\frac{1}{15}$
12) $\frac{1}{12}$
13) $\frac{1}{54}$
14) $\frac{19}{30}$
15) $\frac{27}{56}$
16) $\frac{21}{52}$
17) $\frac{1}{6}$
18) $\frac{7}{2} = 3\frac{1}{2}$
19) $\frac{1}{15}$
20) $\frac{13}{18}$
21) $3\frac{3}{5}$
22) $7\frac{8}{9}$
23) $3\frac{7}{8}$
24) $6\frac{1}{3}$
25) $7\frac{2}{45}$
26) $8\frac{10}{77}$
27) $\frac{2}{3}$
28) $3\frac{2}{5}$
29) $1\frac{1}{9}$
30) $3\frac{1}{6}$
31) $2\frac{5}{7}$
32) $1\frac{5}{42}$
33) $1\frac{11}{20}$
34) $4\frac{7}{60}$
35) $3\frac{9}{14}$
36) $2\frac{4}{5}$
37) $8\frac{1}{4}$
38) $4\frac{4}{35}$
39) $12\frac{1}{10}$
40) 12
41) $14\frac{2}{5}$
42) $22\frac{1}{20}$
43) $\frac{4}{5}$
44) $1\frac{1}{2}$
45) $1\frac{11}{21}$
46) $2\frac{58}{63}$
47) $1\frac{23}{40}$
48) $1\frac{7}{33}$
49) $1\frac{11}{16}$
50) $1\frac{5}{99}$

CHAPTER

2 Decimals

Math topics that you'll learn in this chapter:

- ☑ Comparing Decimals
- ☑ Rounding Decimals
- ☑ Adding and Subtracting Decimals
- ☑ Multiplying and Dividing Decimals

Comparing Decimals

- A decimal is a fraction written in a special form. For example, instead of writing $\frac{1}{2}$ you can write: 0.5
- A Decimal Number contains a Decimal Point. It separates the whole number part from the fractional part of a decimal number.
- Let's review decimal place values: Example: **45.3861**

4: tens	5: ones	3: tenths
8: hundredths	6: thousandths	1: tens thousandths

- To compare two decimals, compare each digit of two decimals in the same place value. Start from left. Compare hundreds, tens, ones, tenth, hundredth, etc.
- To compare numbers, use these symbols:

Equal to $=$	Less than $<$	Greater than $>$
Greater than or equal $\geq$	Less than or equal $\leq$	

Examples:

Example 1. Compare 0.03 and 0.30.

Solution: 0.30 *is greater than* 0.03, because the tenth place of 0.30 is 3, but the tenth place of 0.03 is zero. Then: $0.03 < 0.30$

Example 2. Compare 0.0917 and 0.217.

Solution: 0.217 *is greater than* 0.0917, because the tenth place of 0.217 is 2, but the tenth place of 0.0917 is zero. Then: $0.0917 < 0.217$

Rounding Decimals

- We can round decimals to a certain accuracy or number of decimal places. This is used to make calculations easier to do and results easier to understand when exact values are not too important.
- First, you'll need to remember your place values: For example: **12.4869**

1: tens	2: ones	4: tenths
8: hundredths	6: thousandths	9: tens thousandths

- To round a decimal, first find the place value you'll round to.
- Find the digit to the right of the place value you're rounding to. If it is 5 or bigger, add 1 to the place value you're rounding to and remove all digits on its right side. If the digit to the right of the place value is less than 5, keep the place value and remove all digits on the right.

Examples:

Example 1. Round 4.3679 to the thousandth place value.

Solution: First, look at the next place value to the right, (tens thousandths). It's 9 and it is greater than 5. Thus add 1 to the digit in the thousandth place. The thousandth place is 7. $\rightarrow 7 + 1 = 8$, then, the answer is 4.368

Example 2. Round 1.5237 to the nearest hundredth.

Solution: First, look at the digit to the right of hundredth (thousandths place value). It's 3 and it is less than 5, thus remove all the digits to the right of hundredth place. Then, the answer is 1.52

Adding and Subtracting Decimals

- Line up the decimal numbers.
- Add zeros to have the same number of digits for both numbers if necessary.
- Remember your place values: For example: 73.5196

7: tens	3: ones	5: tenths
1: hundredths	9: thousandths	6: tens thousandths

- Add or subtract using column addition or subtraction.

Examples:

Example 1. Add. $1.7 + 4.12$

Solution: First, line up the numbers: $\begin{array}{r} 1.7 \\ +\,4.12 \\ \hline \end{array}$ $\rightarrow$ Add a zero to have the same number of digits for both numbers. $\begin{array}{r} 1.70 \\ +\,4.12 \\ \hline \end{array}$ $\rightarrow$ Start with the hundredths place: $0 + 2 = 2$, $\begin{array}{r} 1.70 \\ +\,4.12 \\ \hline 2 \end{array}$ $\rightarrow$ Continue with tenths place: $7 + 1 = 8$, $\begin{array}{r} 1.70 \\ +\,4.12 \\ \hline .82 \end{array}$ $\rightarrow$ Add the ones place: $4 + 1 = 5$, $\begin{array}{r} 1.70 \\ +\,4.12 \\ \hline 5.82 \end{array}$ The answer is 5.82.

Example 2. Find the difference. $5.58 - 4.23$

Solution: First, line up the numbers: $\begin{array}{r} 5.58 \\ -\,4.23 \\ \hline \end{array}$ $\rightarrow$ Start with the hundredths place: $8 - 3 = 5$, $\begin{array}{r} 5.58 \\ -\,4.23 \\ \hline 5 \end{array}$ $\rightarrow$ Continue with tenths place. $5 - 2 = 3$, $\begin{array}{r} 5.58 \\ -\,4.23 \\ \hline .35 \end{array}$ $\rightarrow$ Subtract the ones place. $5 - 4 = 1$, $\begin{array}{r} 5.58 \\ -\,4.23 \\ \hline 1.35 \end{array}$

Multiplying and Dividing Decimals

For multiplying decimals:

- Ignore the decimal point and set up and multiply the numbers as you do with whole numbers.
- Count the total number of decimal places in both of the factors.
- Place the decimal point in the product.

For dividing decimals:

- If the divisor is not a whole number, move the decimal point to the right to make it a whole number. Do the same for the dividend.
- Divide similar to whole numbers.

Examples:

Example 1. Find the product. $0.65 \times 0.24 =$

Solution: Set up and multiply the numbers as you do with whole numbers. Line up the numbers: $\begin{array}{r} 65 \\ \underline{\times 24} \end{array}$ $\rightarrow$ Start with the ones place then continue with other digits $\rightarrow \begin{array}{r} 65 \\ \underline{\times 24} \\ 1{,}560 \end{array}$. Count the total number of decimal places in both of the factors. There are four decimals digits. (two for each factor 0.65 and 0.24) Then: $0.65 \times 0.24 = 0.1560 = 0.156$

Example 2. Find the quotient. $1.20 \div 0.4 =$

Solution: The divisor is not a whole number. Multiply it by 10 to get 4: $\rightarrow 0.4 \times 10 = 4$

Do the same for the dividend to get 12. $\rightarrow 1.20 \times 10 = 12$

Now, divide $12 \div 4 = 3$. The answer is 3.

Chapter 2: Practices

Compare. Use >, =, and <

1) 0.5 □ 0.6
2) 0.9 □ 0.8
3) 0.1 □ 0.2
4) 0.02 □ 0.06
5) 0.05 □ 0.08
6) 0.12 □ 0.09
7) 3.2 □ 2.5
8) 4.8 □ 8.4
9) 0.005 □ 0.05
10) 2.02 □ 20.020
11) 55.100 □ 55.10
12) 0.44 □ 0.440
13) 6.01 □ 6.0100
14) 0.77 □ 77.0

Round each decimal to the nearest whole number.

15) 5.8
16) 6.4
17) 12.3
18) 9.2
19) 7.6
20) 22.4
21) 6.8
22) 15.9
23) 13.41
24) 16.78
25) 67.58
26) 42.67
27) 55.89
28) 14.32
29) 78.88
30) 98.29

Find the sum or difference.

31) $12.1 + 36.2 =$

32) $56.3 - 22.2 =$

33) $45.1 + 12.8 =$

34) $27.9 - 16.4 =$

35) $98.8 - 56.6 =$

36) $28.45 + 13.22 =$

37) $16.78 + 45.11 =$

38) $86.16 - 72.12 =$

39) $96.23 - 28.32 =$

40) $57.33 + 67.46 =$

41) $46.26 - 39.49 =$

42) $44.95 + 76.53 =$

43) $79.37 - 52.89 =$

44) $19.99 + 28.7 =$

45) $83.48 - 49.3 =$

46) $19.6 + 42.98 =$

Find the product or quotient.

47) $3.3 \times 0.2 =$

48) $2.4 \div 0.3 =$

49) $8.1 \times 1.4 =$

50) $4.8 \div 0.2 =$

51) $4.1 \times 0.3 =$

52) $8.6 \div 0.2 =$

53) $9.9 \times 0.8 =$

54) $1.84 \div 0.2 =$

55) $2.1 \times 8.4 =$

56) $1.6 \times 4.5 =$

57) $9.2 \times 3.1 =$

58) $36.6 \div 1.6 =$

59) $1.91 \times 5.2 =$

60) $3.65 \times 1.4 =$

61) $24.82 \div 0.4 =$

62) $12.4 \times 4.20 =$

Chapter 2: Answers

1) <
2) >
3) <
4) <
5) <
6) >
7) >
8) <
9) <
10) <
11) =
12) =
13) =
14) <
15) 6
16) 6
17) 12
18) 9
19) 8
20) 22
21) 7
22) 16
23) 13
24) 17
25) 68
26) 43
27) 56
28) 14
29) 79
30) 98
31) 48.3
32) 34.1
33) 57.9
34) 11.5
35) 42.2
36) 41.67
37) 61.89
38) 14.04
39) 67.91
40) 124.79
41) 6.77
42) 121.48
43) 26.48
44) 48.69
45) 34.18
46) 62.58
47) 0.66
48) 8
49) 11.34
50) 24
51) 1.23
52) 43
53) 7.92
54) 9.2
55) 17.64
56) 7.2
57) 28.52
58) 22.875
59) 9.932
60) 5.11
61) 62.05
62) 52.08

CHAPTER

3 Integers and Order of Operations

Math topics that you'll learn in this chapter:

- ☑ Adding and Subtracting Integers
- ☑ Multiplying and Dividing Integers
- ☑ Order of Operations
- ☑ Integers and Absolute Value

Adding and Subtracting Integers

- Integers include zero, counting numbers, and the negative of the counting numbers. $\{\dots, -3, -2, -1, 0, 1, 2, 3, \dots\}$
- Add a positive integer by moving to the right on the number line. (you will get a bigger number)
- Add a negative integer by moving to the left on the number line. (you will get a smaller number)
- Subtract an integer by adding its opposite.

Number line

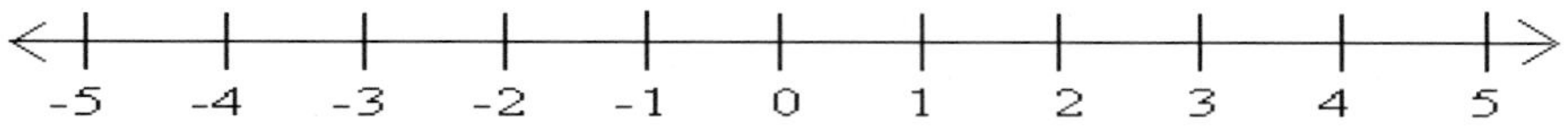

Examples:

Example 1. Solve. $(-2) - (-8) =$

Solution: Keep the first number and convert the sign of the second number to its opposite. (change subtraction into addition. Then: $(-2) + 8 = 6$

Example 2. Solve. $4 + (5 - 10) =$

Solution: First, subtract the numbers in brackets, $5 - 10 = -5$.
Then: $4 + (-5) = \rightarrow$ change addition into subtraction: $4 - 5 = -1$

Example 3. Solve. $(9 - 14) + 15 =$

Solution: First, subtract the numbers in brackets, $9 - 14 = -5$
Then: $-5 + 15 = \rightarrow -5 + 15 = 10$

Example 4. Solve. $12 + (-3 - 10) =$

Solution: First, subtract the numbers in brackets, $-3 - 10 = -13$
Then: $12 + (-13) = \rightarrow$ change addition into subtraction: $12 - 13 = -1$

Find more at bit.ly/3aKx5vl

Multiplying and Dividing Integers

Use the following rules for multiplying and dividing integers:

- (negative) × (negative) = positive
- (negative) ÷ (negative) = positive
- (negative) × (positive) = negative
- (negative) ÷ (positive) = negative
- (positive) × (positive) = positive
- (positive) ÷ (negative) = negative

Examples:

Example 1. Solve. $3 \times (-4) =$

Solution: Use this rule: (positive) × (negative) = negative.
Then: $(3) \times (-4) = -12$

Example 2. Solve. $(-3) + (-24 \div 3) =$

Solution: First, divide -24 by 3, the numbers in brackets, use this rule: (negative) ÷ (positive) = negative. Then: $-24 \div 3 = -8$
$(-3) + (-24 \div 3) = (-3) + (-8) = -3 - 8 = -11$

Example 3. Solve. $(12 - 15) \times (-2) =$

Solution: First, subtract the numbers in brackets,
$12 - 15 = -3 \rightarrow (-3) \times (-2) =$
Now use this rule: (negative) × (negative) = positive $\rightarrow (-3) \times (-2) = 6$

Example 4. Solve. $(12 - 8) \div (-4) =$

Solution: First, subtract the numbers in brackets,
$12 - 8 = 4 \rightarrow (4) \div (-4) =$
Now use this rule: (positive) ÷ (negative) = negative $\rightarrow (4) \div (-4) = -1$

Order of Operations

- In Mathematics, "operations" are addition, subtraction, multiplication, division, exponentiation (written as b^n), and grouping.
- When there is more than one math operation in an expression, use PEMDAS: (to memorize this rule, remember the phrase "Please Excuse My Dear Aunt Sally".)
  - Parentheses
  - Exponents
  - Multiplication and Division (from left to right)
  - Addition and Subtraction (from left to right)

Examples:

Example 1. Calculate. $(2 + 6) \div (2^2 \div 4) =$

Solution: First, simplify inside parentheses:
$(8) \div (4 \div 4) = (8) \div (1)$, Then: $(8) \div (1) = 8$

Example 2. Solve. $(6 \times 5) - (14 - 5) =$

Solution: First, calculate within parentheses: $(6 \times 5) - (14 - 5) = (30) - (9)$, Then: $(30) - (9) = 21$

Example 3. Calculate. $-4[(3 \times 6) \div (9 \times 2)] =$

Solution: First, calculate within parentheses:
$-4[(18) \div (9 \times 2)] = -4[(18) \div (18)] = -4[1]$
multiply -4 and 1. Then: $-4[1] = -4$

Example 4. Solve. $(28 \div 7) + (-19 + 3) =$

Solution: First, calculate within parentheses:
$(28 \div 7) + (-19 + 3) = (4) + (-16)$ Then: $(4) - (16) = -12$

Integers and Absolute Value

- The absolute value of a number is its distance from zero, in either direction, on the number line. For example, the distance of 9 and -9 from zero on number line is 9.
- The absolute value of an integer is the numerical value without its sign. (negative or positive)
- The vertical bar is used for absolute value as in $|x|$.
- The absolute value of a number is never negative; because it only shows, "how far the number is from zero".

Examples:

Example 1. Calculate. $|14-2| \times 5 =$

Solution: First, solve $|14-2|$, $\rightarrow |14-2| = |12|$, the absolute value of 12 is 12, $|12| = 12$, Then: $12 \times 5 = 60$

Example 2. Solve. $\frac{|-24|}{4} \times |5-7| =$

Solution: First, find $|-24| \rightarrow$ the absolute value of -24 is 24. Then: $|-24| = 24$, $\frac{24}{4} \times |5-7| =$

Now, calculate $|5-7|$, $\rightarrow |5-7| = |-2|$, the absolute value of -2 is 2. $|-2| = 2$
Then: $\frac{24}{4} \times 2 = 6 \times 2 = 12$

Example 3. Solve. $|8-2| \times \frac{|-4\times7|}{2} =$

Solution: First, calculate $|8-2|$,$\rightarrow |8-2| = |6|$, the absolute value of 6 is 6, $|6| = 6$. Then: $6 \times \frac{|-4\times7|}{2}$

Now calculate $|-4\times7|$, $\rightarrow |-4\times7| = |-28|$, the absolute value of -28 is 28, $|-28| = 28$, Then: $6 \times \frac{28}{2} = 6 \times 14 = 84$

Chapter 3: Practices

Find each sum or difference.

1) $-9+16=$
2) $-18-6=$
3) $-24+10=$
4) $30+(-5)=$
5) $15+(-3)=$
6) $(-13)+(-4)=$
7) $25+(3-10)=$
8) $12-(-6+9)=$
9) $5-(-2+7)=$
10) $(-11)+(-5+6)=$
11) $(-3)+(9-16)=$
12) $(-8)-(13+4)=$
13) $(-7+9)-39=$
14) $(-30+6)-14=$
15) $(-5+9)+(-3+7)=$
16) $(8-19)-(-4+12)=$
17) $(-9+2)-(6-7)=$
18) $(-12-5)-(-4-14)=$

Solve.

19) $3\times(-6)=$
20) $(-32)\div 4=$
21) $(-5)\times 4=$
22) $(25)\div(-5)=$
23) $(-72)\div 8=$
24) $(-2)\times(-6)\times 5=$
25) $(-2)\times 3\times(-7)=$
26) $(-1)\times(-3)\times(-5)=$
27) $(-2)\times(-3)\times(-6)=$
28) $(-12+3)\times(-5)=$
29) $(-3+4)\times(-11)=$
30) $(-9)\times(6-5)=$
31) $(-3-7)\times(-6)=$
32) $(-7+3)\times(-9+6)=$
33) $(-15)\div(-17+12)=$
34) $(-3-2)\times(-9+7)=$
35) $(-15+31)\div(-2)=$
36) $(-64)\div(-16+8)=$

Evaluate each expression.

37) $3 + (2 \times 5) =$

38) $(5 \times 4) - 7 =$

39) $(-9 \times 2) + 6 =$

40) $(7 \times 3) - (-5) =$

41) $(-8) + (2 \times 7) =$

42) $(9 - 6) + (3 \times 4) =$

43) $(-19 + 5) + (6 \times 2) =$

44) $(32 \div 4) + (1 - 13) =$

45) $(-36 \div 6) - (12 + 3) =$

46) $(-16 + 5) - (54 \div 9) =$

47) $(-20 + 4) - (35 \div 5) =$

48) $(42 \div 7) + (2 \times 3) =$

49) $(28 \div 4) + (2 \times 6) =$

50) $2[(3 \times 3) - (4 \times 5)] =$

51) $3[(2 \times 8) + (4 \times 3)] =$

52) $2[(9 \times 3) - (6 \times 4)] =$

53) $4[(4 \times 8) \div (4 \times 4)] =$

54) $-5[(10 \times 8) \div (5 \times 8)] =$

Find the answers.

55) $|-5| + |7 - 10| =$

56) $|-4 + 6| + |-2| =$

57) $|-9| + |1 - 9| =$

58) $|-7| - |8 - 12| =$

59) $|9 - 11| + |8 - 15| =$

60) $|-7 + 10| - |-8 + 3| =$

61) $|-12 + 6| - |3 - 9| =$

62) $5 + |2 - 6| + |3 - 4| =$

63) $-4 + |2 - 6| + |1 - 9| =$

64) $|-6| \times |-7| + |2 - 8| =$

65) $|-12| \times |-3| + |4 - 28| =$

66) $|4 \times (-2)| \times |-9| =$

67) $|-3 \times 2| \times |-5| =$

68) $|3 - 12| - |-3 \times 7| =$

69) $|-9| + |-7 \times 5| =$

70) $|-11| + |-6 \times 4| =$

71) $|-4 \times 2 + 6| \times |-2 \times 8| =$

72) $|-1 \times 5 + 2| \times |-4| =$

Chapter 3: Answers

1) 7
2) −24
3) −14
4) 25
5) 12
6) −17
7) 18
8) 9
9) 0
10) −10
11) −10
12) −25
13) −37
14) −38
15) 8
16) −19
17) −6
18) 1
19) −18
20) −8
21) −20
22) −5
23) −9
24) 60
25) 42
26) −15
27) −36
28) 45
29) −11
30) −9
31) 60
32) 12
33) 3
34) 10
35) −8
36) 8
37) 13
38) 13
39) −12
40) 26
41) 6
42) 15
43) −2
44) −4
45) −21
46) −17
47) −23
48) 12
49) 19
50) −22
51) 84
52) 6
53) 8
54) −10
55) 8
56) 4
57) 17
58) 3
59) 9
60) −2
61) 0
62) 10
63) 8
64) 48
65) 60
66) 72
67) 30
68) −12
69) 44
70) 35
71) 32
72) 12

CHAPTER

4 Ratios and Proportions

Math topics that you'll learn in this chapter:

- ☑ Simplifying Ratios
- ☑ Proportional Ratios
- ☑ Similarity and Ratios

Simplifying Ratios

- Ratios are used to make comparisons between two numbers.
- Ratios can be written as a fraction, using the word "to", or with a colon. Example: $\frac{3}{4}$ or "3 to 4" or 3:4
- You can calculate equivalent ratios by multiplying or dividing both sides of the ratio by the same number.

Examples:

Example 1. Simplify. $8:2 =$

Solution: Both numbers 8 and 2 are divisible by $2 \Rightarrow 8 \div 2 = 4$, $4 \div 2 = 2$, Then: $8:2 = 4:1$

Example 2. Simplify. $\frac{9}{33} =$

Solution: Both numbers 9 and 33 are divisible by $3 \Rightarrow 33 \div 3 = 11$, $9 \div 3 = 3$, Then: $\frac{9}{33} = \frac{3}{11}$

Example 3. There are 24 students in a class and 10 are girls. Find the ratio of girls to boys in that class.

Solution: Subtract 10 from 24 to find the number of boys in the class.
$24 - 10 = 14$. There are 14 boys in the class. So, the ratio of girls to boys is $10:14$.
Now, simplify this ratio. Both 14 and 10 are divisible by 2.
Then: $14 \div 2 = 7$, and $10 \div 2 = 5$. In the simplest form, this ratio is $5:7$

Example 4. A recipe calls for butter and sugar in the ratio $3:4$. If you're using 9 cups of butter, how many cups of sugar should you use?

Solution: Since you use 9 cups of butter, or 3 times as much, you need to multiply the amount of sugar by 3. Then: $4 \times 3 = 12$. So, you need to use 12 cups of sugar. You can solve this using equivalent fractions: $\frac{3}{4} = \frac{9}{12}$

Proportional Ratios

- Two ratios are proportional if they represent the same relationship.
- A proportion means that two ratios are equal. It can be written in two ways: $\frac{a}{b} = \frac{c}{d}$ $\qquad a : b = c : d$
- The proportion $\frac{a}{b} = \frac{c}{d}$ can be written as: $a \times d = c \times b$

Examples:

Example 1. Solve this proportion for x. $\quad \frac{2}{5} = \frac{6}{x}$

Solution: Use cross multiplication: $\frac{2}{5} = \frac{6}{x} \Rightarrow 2 \times x = 6 \times 5 \Rightarrow 2x = 30$

Divide both sides by 2 to find x: $x = \frac{30}{2} \Rightarrow x = 15$

Example 2. If a box contains red and blue balls in ratio of 3: 5 red to blue, how many red balls are there if 45 blue balls are in the box?

Solution: Write a proportion and solve. $\frac{3}{5} = \frac{x}{45}$

Use cross multiplication: $3 \times 45 = 5 \times x \Rightarrow 135 = 5x$

Divide to find x: $\quad x = \frac{135}{5} \Rightarrow x = 27$. There are 27 red balls in the box.

Example 3. Solve this proportion for x. $\quad \frac{4}{9} = \frac{16}{x}$

Solution: Use cross multiplication: $\quad \frac{4}{9} = \frac{16}{x} \Rightarrow 4 \times x = 9 \times 16 \Rightarrow 4x = 144$

Divide to find x: $\quad x = \frac{144}{4} \Rightarrow x = 36$

Example 4. Solve this proportion for x. $\frac{5}{7} = \frac{20}{x}$

Solution: Use cross multiplication: $\quad \frac{5}{7} = \frac{20}{x} \Rightarrow 5 \times x = 7 \times 20 \Rightarrow 5x = 140$

Divide to find x: $\quad x = \frac{140}{5} \Rightarrow x = 28$

Similarity and Ratios

- Two figures are similar if they have the same shape.
- Two or more figures are similar if the corresponding angles are equal, and the corresponding sides are in proportion.

Examples:

Example 1. The following triangles are similar. What is the value of the unknown side?

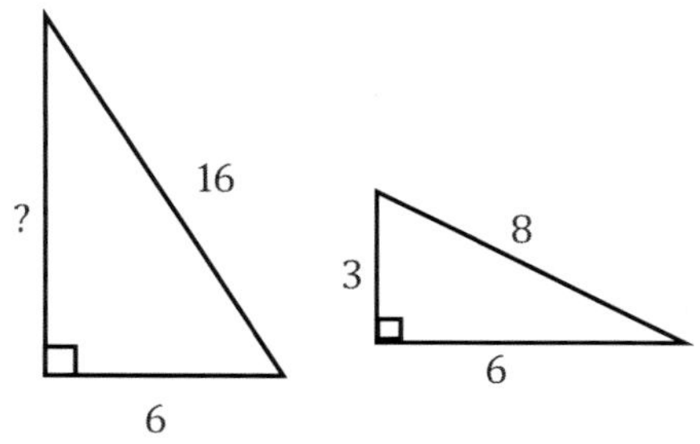

Solution: Find the corresponding sides and write a proportion.

$\frac{8}{16}=\frac{6}{x}$. Now, use the cross product to solve for x:

$\frac{8}{16}=\frac{6}{x} \rightarrow 8\times x=16\times 6 \rightarrow 8x=96$. Divide both sides by 8. Then: $8x=96 \rightarrow x=\frac{96}{8} \rightarrow x=12$

The missing side is 12.

Example 2. Two rectangles are similar. The first is 5 feet wide and 15 feet long. The second is 10 feet wide. What is the length of the second rectangle?

Solution: Let's put x for the length of the second rectangle. Since two rectangles are similar, their corresponding sides are in proportion. Write a proportion and solve for the missing number.

$\frac{5}{10}=\frac{15}{x} \rightarrow 5x=10\times 15 \rightarrow 5x=150 \rightarrow x=\frac{150}{5}=30$

The length of the second rectangle is 30 feet.

bit.ly/2KKKmcV

Find more at

Chapter 4: Practices

Reduce each ratio.

1) 2: 18 = ___:___
2) 5: 35 = ___:___
3) 8: 72 = ___:___
4) 24: 36 = ___:___
5) 25: 40 = ___:___
6) 40: 72 = ___:___
7) 28: 63 = ___:___
8) 18: 81 = ___:___
9) 13: 52 = ___:___
10) 56: 72 = ___:___
11) 42: 63 = ___:___
12) 32: 96 = ___:___

Solve.

13) Bob has 16 red cards and 20 green cards. What is the ratio of Bob's red cards to his green cards? ________

14) In a party, 34 soft drinks are required for every 20 guests. If there are 260 guests, how many soft drinks are required? ________

15) Sara has 56 blue pens and 28 black pens. What is the ratio of Sara's black pens to her blue pens? ________

16) In Jack's class, 48 of the students are tall and 20 are short. In Michael's class 28 students are tall and 12 students are short. Which class has a higher ratio of tall to short students? ________

17) The price of 6 apples at the Quick Market is $1.52. The price of 5 of the same apples at Walmart is $1.32. Which place is the better buy? _______

18) The bakers at a Bakery can make 180 bagels in 6 hours. How many bagels can they bake in 16 hours? What is that rate per hour? ________

19) You can buy 6 cans of green beans at a supermarket for $3.48. How much does it cost to buy 38 cans of green beans? ________

Solve each proportion.

20) $\frac{3}{2} = \frac{9}{x} \Rightarrow x =$ ____

21) $\frac{7}{2} = \frac{x}{4} \Rightarrow x =$ ____

22) $\frac{1}{3} = \frac{2}{x} \Rightarrow x =$ ____

23) $\frac{1}{4} = \frac{5}{x} \Rightarrow x =$ ____

24) $\frac{9}{6} = \frac{x}{2} \Rightarrow x =$ ____

25) $\frac{3}{6} = \frac{5}{x} \Rightarrow x =$ ____

26) $\frac{7}{x} = \frac{2}{6} \Rightarrow x =$ ____

27) $\frac{2}{x} = \frac{4}{10} \Rightarrow x =$ ____

28) $\frac{3}{2} = \frac{x}{8} \Rightarrow x =$ ____

29) $\frac{x}{6} = \frac{5}{3} \Rightarrow x =$ ____

30) $\frac{3}{9} = \frac{5}{x} \Rightarrow x =$ ____

31) $\frac{4}{18} = \frac{2}{x} \Rightarrow x =$ ____

32) $\frac{6}{16} = \frac{3}{x} \Rightarrow x =$ ____

33) $\frac{2}{5} = \frac{x}{20} \Rightarrow x =$ ____

34) $\frac{28}{8} = \frac{x}{2} \Rightarrow x =$ ____

35) $\frac{3}{5} = \frac{x}{15} \Rightarrow x =$ ____

36) $\frac{2}{7} = \frac{x}{14} \Rightarrow x =$ ____

37) $\frac{x}{18} = \frac{3}{2} \Rightarrow x =$ ____

38) $\frac{x}{24} = \frac{2}{6} \Rightarrow x =$ ____

39) $\frac{5}{x} = \frac{4}{20} \Rightarrow x =$ ____

40) $\frac{10}{x} = \frac{20}{80} \Rightarrow x =$ ____

41) $\frac{90}{6} = \frac{x}{2} \Rightarrow x =$ ____

Solve each problem.

42) Two rectangles are similar. The first is $8\,feet$ wide and $32\,feet$ long. The second is $12\,feet$ wide. What is the length of the second rectangle?

____

43) Two rectangles are similar. One is $4.6\,meters$ by $7\,meters$. The longer side of the second rectangle is $28\,meters$. What is the other side of the second rectangle? ________________

Chapter 4: Answers

1) 1: 9
2) 1: 7
3) 1: 9
4) 2: 3
5) 5: 8
6) 5: 9
7) 4: 9
8) 2: 9
9) 1: 4
10) 7: 9
11) 2: 3
12) 1: 3
13) 4: 5
14) 442
15) 1: 2

16) $Jack's\ class: \frac{48}{20} = \frac{12}{5}$ $Michael's\ class: \frac{28}{12} = \frac{7}{3}$ Jack's class has a higher ratio of tall to short student: $\frac{12}{5} > \frac{7}{3}$

17) Quick market
18) 480, 30 bagels per hour
19) $22.04
20) 6
21) 14
22) 6
23) 20
24) 3
25) 10
26) 21
27) 5
28) 12
29) 10
30) 15
31) 9
32) 8
33) 8
34) 7
35) 9
36) 4
37) 27
38) 8
39) 25
40) 40
41) 30
42) 48 $feet$
43) 18.4 $meters$

CHAPTER

5 Percentage

Math topics that you'll learn in this chapter:

- ☑ Percent Problems
- ☑ Percent of Increase and Decrease
- ☑ Discount, Tax and Tip
- ☑ Simple Interest

Percent Problems

- Percent is a ratio of a number and 100. It always has the same denominator, 100. The percent symbol is "%".
- Percent means "per 100". So, 20% is $\frac{20}{100}$.
- In each percent problem, we are looking for the base, or the part or the percent.
- Use these equations to find each missing section in a percent problem:
  - Base = Part ÷ Percent
  - Part = Percent × Base
  - Percent = Part ÷ Base

Examples:

Example 1. What is 20% of 40?

Solution: In this problem, we have the percent (20%) and the base (40) and we are looking for the "part". Use this formula: $Part = Percent \times Base$.
Then: $Part = 20\% \times 40 = \frac{20}{100} \times 40 = 0.20 \times 40 = 8$. The answer: 20% of 40 is 8.

Example 2. 25 is what percent of 500?

Solution: In this problem, we are looking for the percent. Use this equation:
$Percent = Part \div Base \rightarrow Percent = 25 \div 500 = 0.05 = 5\%$.
Then: 25 is 5 percent of 500.

Example 3. 80 is 20 percent of what number?

Solution: In this problem, we are looking for the base. Use this equation:
$Base = Part \div Percent \rightarrow Base = 80 \div 20\% = 80 \div 0.20 = 400$
Then: 80 is 20 percent of 400.

Percent of Increase and Decrease

- Percent of change (increase or decrease) is a mathematical concept that represents the degree of change over time.
- To find the percentage of increase or decrease:
  1. New Number – Original Number
  2. (The result ÷ Original Number) × 100
- Or use this formula: Percent of change $= \frac{new\ number - original\ number}{original\ number} \times 100$
- Note: If your answer is a negative number, then this is a percentage decrease. If it is positive, then this is a percentage increase.

Examples:

Example 1. The price of a shirt increases from \$30 to \$36. What is the percentage increase?

Solution: First, find the difference: $36 - 30 = 6$

Then: $(6 \div 30) \times 100 = \frac{6}{30} \times 100 = 20$. The percentage increase is 20%. It means that the price of the shirt increased by 20%.

Example 2. The price of a table decreased from \$50 to \$35. What is the percent of decrease?

Solution: Use this formula:

$Percent\ of\ change = \frac{new\ number - original\ number}{original\ number} \times 100 =$

$\frac{35-50}{50} \times 100 = \frac{-15}{50} \times 100 = -30$. The percentage decrease is 30. (the negative sign means percentage decrease) Therefore, the price of the table decreased by 30%.

Discount, Tax and Tip

- To find the discount: Multiply the regular price by the rate of discount
- To find the selling price: Original price – discount
- To find tax: Multiply the tax rate to the taxable amount (income, property value, etc.)
- To find the tip, multiply the rate to the selling price.

Examples:

Example 1. With an 20% discount, Ella saved \$50 on a dress. What was the original price of the dress?

Solution: let x be the original price of the dress. Then: $20\ \%\ of\ x = 50$. Write an equation and solve for x: $0.20 \times x = 50 \rightarrow x = \frac{50}{0.20} = 250$. The original price of the dress was \$250.

Example 2. Sophia purchased a new computer for a price of \$820 at the Apple Store. What is the total amount her credit card is charged if the sales tax is 5%?

Solution: The taxable amount is \$820, and the tax rate is 5%. Then:

$$Tax = 0.05 \times 820 = 41$$

$Final\ price = Selling\ price + Tax \rightarrow final\ price = \$820 + \$41 = \$861$

Example 3. Nicole and her friends went out to eat at a restaurant. If their bill was \$60.00 and they gave their server a 15% tip, how much did they pay altogether?

Solution: First, find the tip. To find the tip, multiply the rate to the bill amount. $Tip = 60 \times 0.15 = 9$. The final price is: $\$60 + \$9 = \$69$

Simple Interest

- Simple Interest: The charge for borrowing money or the return for lending it.
- Simple interest is calculated on the initial amount (principal).
- To solve a simple interest problem, use this formula:

$Interest = principal \times rate \times time \qquad (I = p \times r \times t = prt)$

Examples:

Example 1. Find simple interest for \$200 investment at 5% for 3 years.

Solution: Use Interest formula:
$I = prt$ $(P = \$200,\ r = 5\% = \frac{5}{100} = 0.05$ and $t = 3)$
Then: $I = 200 \times 0.05 \times 3 = \$30$

Example 2. Find simple interest for \$1,200 at 8% for 6 years.

Solution: Use Interest formula:
$I = prt$ $(P = \$1{,}200,\ r = 8\% = \frac{8}{100} = 0.08$ and $t = 6)$
Then: $I = 1{,}200 \times 0.08 \times 6 = \$576$

Example 3. Andy received a student loan to pay for his educational expenses this year. What is the interest on the loan if he borrowed \$4,500 at 6% for 5 years?

Solution: Use Interest formula: $I = prt$. $P = \$4{,}500$, $r = 6\% = 0.06$ and $t = 5$
Then: $I = 4{,}500 \times 0.06 \times 5 = \$1{,}350$

Example 4. Bob is starting his own small business. He borrowed \$20,000 from the bank at an 8% rate for 6 months. Find the interest Bob will pay on this loan.

Solution: Use Interest formula:
$I = prt$. $P = \$20{,}000$, $r = 8\% = 0.08$ and $t = 0.5$ (6 months is half year). Then:

$$I = 20{,}000 \times 0.08 \times 0.5 = \$800$$

Find more at bit.ly/3nJIi3D

Chapter 5: Practices

Solve each problem.

1) What is 15% of 60? ____
2) What is 55% of 800? ____
3) What is 22% of 120? ____
4) What is 18% of 40? ____
5) 90 is what percent of 200? ____%
6) 30 is what percent of 150? ____%
7) 14 is what percent of 250? ____%
8) 60 is what percent of 300? ____%
9) 30 is 120 percent of what number? ____
10) 120 is 20 percent of what number? ____
11) 15 is 5 percent of what number? ____
12) 22 is 20% of what number? ____

Solve each problem.

13) Bob got a raise, and his hourly wage increased from $15 to $21. What is the percent increase? _____ %
14) The price of a pair of shoes increases from $32 to $36. What is the percent increase? ___ %
15) At a coffee shop, the price of a cup of coffee increased from $1.35 to $1.62. What is the percent increase in the cost of the coffee? _____ %
16) A $45 shirt now selling for $36 is discounted by what percent? _____ %
17) Joe scored 30 out of 35 marks in Algebra, 20 out of 30 marks in science and 58 out of 70 marks in mathematics. In which subject his percentage of marks is best? _____
18) Emma purchased a computer for $420. The computer is regularly priced at $480. What was the percent discount Emma received on the computer? _____
19) A chemical solution contains 15% alcohol. If there is 54 ml of alcohol, what is the volume of the solution? _____

Find the selling price of each item.

20) Original price of a computer: $600

Tax: 8%, Selling price: $_______

21) Original price of a laptop: $450

Tax: 10%, Selling price: $_______

22) Nicolas hired a moving company. The company charged $500 for its services, and Nicolas gives the movers a 14% tip. How much does Nicolas tip the movers? $_________

23) Mason has lunch at a restaurant and the cost of his meal is $40. Mason wants to leave a 20% tip. What is Mason's total bill, including tip? $_________

Determine the simple interest for the following loans.

24) $\$1{,}000$ *at* 5% *for* 4 *years*. $__

25) $400 *at* 3% *for* 5 *years*. $__

26) $240 *at* 4% *for* 3 *years*. $__

27) $500 at 4.5% for 6 years. $__

Solve.

28) A new car, valued at $20,000, depreciates at 8% per year. What is the value of the car one year after purchase? $_____________

29) Sara puts $7,000 into an investment yielding 3% annual simple interest; she left the money in for five years. How much interest does Sara get at the end of those five years? $_____________

Chapter 5: Answers

1) 9
2) 440
3) 26.4
4) 7.2
5) 45%
6) 20%
7) 5.6%
8) 20%
9) 25
10) 600
11) 300
12) 110
13) 40%
14) 12.5%
15) 20%
16) 20%
17) Algebra
18) 12.5%
19) 360 ml
20) $648.00
21) $495.00
22) $70.00
23) $48.00
24) $200.00
25) $60.00
26) $28.80
27) $135.00
28) $18.400
29) $1,050

CHAPTER

6 Exponents and Variables

Math topics that you'll learn in this chapter:

- ☑ Multiplication Property of Exponents
- ☑ Division Property of Exponents
- ☑ Powers of Products and Quotients
- ☑ Zero and Negative Exponents
- ☑ Negative Exponents and Negative Bases
- ☑ Scientific Notation
- ☑ Radicals

Multiplication Property of Exponents

- Exponents are shorthand for repeated multiplication of the same number by itself. For example, instead of 2×2, we can write 2^2. For $3 \times 3 \times 3 \times 3$, we can write 3^4
- In algebra, a variable is a letter used to stand for a number. The most common letters are: x, y, z, a, b, c, m, and n.
- Exponent's rules: $x^a \times x^b = x^{a+b}$, $\frac{x^a}{x^b} = x^{a-b}$

$$(x^a)^b = x^{a \times b} \qquad (xy)^a = x^a \times y^a \qquad \left(\frac{a}{b}\right)^c = \frac{a^c}{b^c}$$

Examples:

Example 1. Multiply. $2x^2 \times 3x^4$

Solution: Use Exponent's rules: $x^a \times x^b = x^{a+b} \rightarrow x^2 \times x^4 = x^{2+4} = x^6$
Then: $2x^2 \times 3x^4 = 6x^6$

Example 2. Simplify. $(x^4y^2)^2$

Solution: Use Exponent's rules: $(x^a)^b = x^{a \times b}$.
Then: $(x^4y^2)^2 = x^{4\times2}y^{2\times2} = x^8y^4$

Example 3. Multiply. $5x^8 \times 6x^5$

Solution: Use Exponent's rules: $x^a \times x^b = x^{a+b} \rightarrow x^8 \times x^5 = x^{8+5} = x^{13}$
Then: $5x^8 \times 6x^5 = 30x^{13}$

Example 4. Simplify. $(x^4y^7)^3$

Solution: Use Exponent's rules: $(x^a)^b = x^{a \times b}$.
Then: $(x^4y^7)^3 = x^{4\times3}y^{7\times3} = x^{12}y^{21}$

Division Property of Exponents

For division of exponents use following formulas:

- $\frac{x^a}{x^b} = x^{a-b}\ (x \neq 0)$
- $\frac{x^a}{x^b} = \frac{1}{x^{b-a}}, \ (x \neq 0)$
- $\frac{1}{x^b} = x^{-b}$

Examples:

Example 1. Simplify. $\frac{16x^3y}{2xy^2} =$

Solution: First, cancel the common factor: $2 \rightarrow \frac{16x^3y}{2xy^2} = \frac{8x^3y}{xy^2}$

Use Exponent's rules: $\frac{x^a}{x^b} = x^{a-b} \ \rightarrow \frac{x^3}{x} = x^{3-1} = x^2$ and $\frac{x^a}{x^b} = \frac{1}{x^{b-a}} \rightarrow \frac{y}{y^2} = \frac{1}{y^{2-1}} = \frac{1}{y}$

Then: $\frac{16x^3y}{2xy^2} = \frac{8x^2}{y}$

Example 2. Simplify. $\frac{24x^8}{3x^6} =$

Solution: Use Exponent's rules: $\frac{x^a}{x^b} = x^{a-b} \ \rightarrow \frac{x^8}{x^6} = x^{8-6} = x^2$

Then: $\frac{24x^8}{3x^6} = 8x^2$

Example 3. Simplify. $\frac{7x^4y^2}{28x^3y} =$

Solution: First, cancel the common factor: $7 \rightarrow \frac{x^4y^2}{4x^3y}$

Use Exponent's rules: $\frac{x^a}{x^b} = x^{a-b} \ \rightarrow \frac{x^4}{x^3} = x^{4-3} = x$ and $\frac{y^2}{y} = y$

Then: $\frac{7x^4y^2}{28x^3y} = \frac{xy}{4}$

Powers of Products and Quotients

- For any nonzero numbers a and b and any integer x, $(ab)^x = a^x \times b^x$ and $\left(\frac{a}{b}\right)^c = \frac{a^c}{b^c}$

Examples:

Example 1. Simplify. $(3x^3y^2)^2$

Solution: Use Exponent's rules: $(x^a)^b = x^{a \times b}$

$(3x^3y^2)^2 = (3)^2(x^3)^2(y^2)^2 = 9x^{3\times2}y^{2\times2} = 9x^6y^4$

Example 2. Simplify. $\left(\frac{2x^3}{3x^2}\right)^2$

Solution: First, cancel the common factor: $x \rightarrow \left(\frac{2x^3}{3x^2}\right) = \left(\frac{2x}{3}\right)^2$

Use Exponent's rules: $\left(\frac{a}{b}\right)^c = \frac{a^c}{b^c}$, Then: $\left(\frac{2x}{3}\right)^2 = \frac{(2x)^2}{(3)^2} = \frac{4x^2}{9}$

Example 3. Simplify. $(-4x^3y^5)^2$

Solution: Use Exponent's rules: $(x^a)^b = x^{a \times b}$

$$(-4x^3y^5)^2 = (-4)^2(x^3)^2(y^5)^2 = 16x^{3\times2}y^{5\times2} = 16x^6y^{10}$$

Example 4. Simplify. $\left(\frac{5x}{4x^2}\right)^2$

Solution: First, cancel the common factor: $x \rightarrow \left(\frac{5x}{4x^2}\right)^2 = \left(\frac{5}{4x}\right)^2$

Use Exponent's rules: $\left(\frac{a}{b}\right)^c = \frac{a^c}{b^c}$, Then: $\left(\frac{5}{4x}\right)^2 = \frac{5^2}{(4x)^2} = \frac{25}{16x^2}$

Zero and Negative Exponents

- Zero-Exponent Rule: $\boldsymbol{a}^0 = 1$, this means that anything raised to the zero power is 1. For example: $(5xy)^0 = 1$ (number zero is an exception: $\mathbf{0}^0 = 0$)
- A negative exponent simply means that the base is on the wrong side of the fraction line, so you need to flip the base to the other side. For instance, "x^{-2}" (pronounced as "ecks to the minus two") just means "x^2" but underneath, as in $\frac{\mathbf{1}}{x^2}$.

Examples:

Example 1. Evaluate. $\left(\frac{4}{5}\right)^{-2} =$

Solution: Use negative exponent's rule: $\left(\frac{x^a}{x^b}\right)^{-2} = \left(\frac{x^b}{x^a}\right)^2 \rightarrow \left(\frac{4}{5}\right)^{-2} = \left(\frac{5}{4}\right)^2$

Then: $\left(\frac{5}{4}\right)^2 = \frac{5^2}{4^2} = \frac{25}{16}$

Example 2. Evaluate. $\left(\frac{3}{2}\right)^{-3} =$

Solution: Use negative exponent's rule: $\left(\frac{x^a}{x^b}\right)^{-3} = \left(\frac{x^b}{x^a}\right)^3 \rightarrow \left(\frac{3}{2}\right)^{-3} = \left(\frac{2}{3}\right)^3 =$

Then: $\left(\frac{2}{3}\right)^3 = \frac{2^3}{3^3} = \frac{8}{27}$

Example 3. Evaluate. $\left(\frac{a}{b}\right)^0 =$

Solution: Use zero-exponent Rule: $\boldsymbol{a}^0 = 1$

Then: $\left(\frac{a}{b}\right)^0 = 1$

Example 4. Evaluate. $\left(\frac{4}{7}\right)^{-1} =$

Solution: Use negative exponent's rule: $\left(\frac{x^a}{x^b}\right)^{-1} = \left(\frac{x^b}{x^a}\right)^1 \rightarrow \left(\frac{4}{7}\right)^{-1} = \left(\frac{7}{4}\right)^1 = \frac{7}{4}$

Find more at bit.ly/3rnkh4v

Negative Exponents and Negative Bases

- A negative exponent is the reciprocal of that number with a positive exponent. $(3)^{-2} = \frac{1}{3^2}$
- To simplify a negative exponent, make the power positive!
- The parenthesis is important! -5^{-2} is not the same as $(-5)^{-2}$

$$-5^{-2} = -\frac{1}{5^2} \text{ and } (-5)^{-2} = +\frac{1}{5^2}$$

Examples:

Example 1. Simplify. $\left(\frac{2a}{3c}\right)^{-2} =$

Solution: Use negative exponent's rule: $\left(\frac{x^a}{x^b}\right)^{-2} = \left(\frac{x^b}{x^a}\right)^2 \rightarrow \left(\frac{2a}{3c}\right)^{-2} = \left(\frac{3c}{2a}\right)^2$

Now use exponent's rule: $\left(\frac{a}{b}\right)^c = \frac{a^c}{b^c} \rightarrow= \left(\frac{3c}{2a}\right)^2 = \frac{3^2c^2}{2^2a^2}$

Then: $\frac{3^2c^2}{2^2a^2} = \frac{9c^2}{4a^2}$

Example 2. Simplify. $\left(\frac{x}{4y}\right)^{-3} =$

Solution: Use negative exponent's rule: $\left(\frac{x^a}{x^b}\right)^{-3} = \left(\frac{x^b}{x^a}\right)^3 \rightarrow \left(\frac{x}{4y}\right)^{-3} = \left(\frac{4y}{x}\right)^3$

Now use exponent's rule: $\left(\frac{a}{b}\right)^c = \frac{a^c}{b^c} \rightarrow \left(\frac{4y}{x}\right)^3 = \frac{4^3y^3}{x^3} = \frac{64y^3}{x^3}$

Example 3. Simplify. $\left(\frac{5a}{2c}\right)^{-2} =$

Solution: Use negative exponent's rule: $\left(\frac{x^a}{x^b}\right)^{-2} = \left(\frac{x^b}{x^a}\right)^2 \rightarrow \left(\frac{5a}{2c}\right)^{-2} = \left(\frac{2c}{5a}\right)^2$

Now use exponent's rule: $\left(\frac{a}{b}\right)^c = \frac{a^c}{b^c} \rightarrow= \left(\frac{2c}{5a}\right)^2 = \frac{2^2c^2}{5^2a^2}$

Then: $\frac{2^2c^2}{5^2a^2} = \frac{4c^2}{25a^2}$

Scientific Notation

- Scientific notation is used to write very big or very small numbers in decimal form.
- In scientific notation, all numbers are written in the form of: $m \times 10^n$, where m is greater than 1 and less than 10.
- To convert a number from scientific notation to standard form, move the decimal point to the left (if the exponent of ten is a negative number), or to the right (if the exponent is positive).

Examples:

Example 1. Write 0.00024 in scientific notation.

Solution: First, move the decimal point to the right so you have a number between 1 and 10. That number is 2.4. Now, determine how many places the decimal moved in step 1 by the power of 10. We moved the decimal point 4 digits to the right. Then: $10^{-4} \rightarrow$ When the decimal moved to the right, the exponent is negative. Then: $0.00024 = 2.4 \times 10^{-4}$

Example 2. Write 3.8×10^{-5} in standard notation.

Solution: The exponent is negative 5. Then, move the decimal point to the left five digits. (remember $3.8 = 0000003.8$) When the decimal moved to the right, the exponent is negative. Then: $3.8 \times 10^{-5} = 0.000038$

Example 3. Write 0.00031 in scientific notation.

Solution: First, move the decimal point to the right so you have a number between 1 and 10. Then: $m = 3.1$, Now, determine how many places the decimal moved in step 1 by the power of 10. $10^{-4} \rightarrow$ Then: $0.00031 = 3.1 \times 10^{-4}$

Example 4. Write 6.2×10^5 in standard notation.

Solution: $10^5 \rightarrow$ The exponent is positive 5. Then, move the decimal point to the right five digits. (remember $6.2 = 6.20000$) Then: $6.2 \times 10^5 = 620{,}000$

bit.ly/3nOwJYP
Find more at

Radicals

- If n is a positive integer and x is a real number, then: $\sqrt[n]{x} = x^{\frac{1}{n}}$,

$$\sqrt[n]{xy} = x^{\frac{1}{n}} \times y^{\frac{1}{n}},\ \sqrt[n]{\frac{x}{y}} = \frac{x^{\frac{1}{n}}}{y^{\frac{1}{n}}},\ \text{and}\ \sqrt[n]{x} \times \sqrt[n]{y} = \sqrt[n]{xy}$$

- A square root of x is a number r whose square is: $r^2 = x$ ($\boldsymbol{r}$ is a square root of x)
- To add and subtract radicals, we need to have the same values under the radical. For example: $\sqrt{3} + \sqrt{3} = 2\sqrt{3}$, $3\sqrt{5} - \sqrt{5} = 2\sqrt{5}$

Examples:

Example 1. Find the square root of $\sqrt{121}$.

Solution: First, factor the number: $121 = 11^2$, Then: $\sqrt{121} = \sqrt{11^2}$,
Now use radical rule: $\sqrt[n]{a^n} = a$. Then: $\sqrt{121} = \sqrt{11^2} = 11$

Example 2. Evaluate. $\sqrt{4} \times \sqrt{16} =$

Solution: Find the values of $\sqrt{4}$ and $\sqrt{16}$. Then: $\sqrt{4} \times \sqrt{16} = 2 \times 4 = 8$

Example 3. Solve. $5\sqrt{2} + 9\sqrt{2}$.

Solution: Since we have the same values under the radical, we can add these two radicals: $5\sqrt{2} + 9\sqrt{2} = 14\sqrt{2}$

Example 4. Evaluate. $\sqrt{2} \times \sqrt{50} =$

Solution: Use this radical rule: $\sqrt[n]{x} \times \sqrt[n]{y} = \sqrt[n]{xy} \rightarrow \sqrt{2} \times \sqrt{50} = \sqrt{100}$
The square root of 100 is 10. Then: $\sqrt{2} \times \sqrt{50} = \sqrt{100} = 10$

Chapter 6: Practices

Find the products.

1) $x^2 \times 4xy^2 =$

2) $3x^2y \times 5x^3y^2 =$

3) $6x^4y^2 \times x^2y^3 =$

4) $7xy^3 \times 2x^2y =$

5) $-5x^5y^5 \times x^3y^2 =$

6) $-8x^3y^2 \times 3x^3y^2 =$

7) $-6x^2y^6 \times 5x^4y^2 =$

8) $-3x^3y^3 \times 2x^3y^2 =$

9) $-6x^5y^3 \times 4x^4y^3 =$

10) $-2x^4y^3 \times 5x^6y^2 =$

11) $-7y^6 \times 3x^6y^3 =$

12) $-9x^4 \times 2x^4y^2 =$

Simplify.

13) $\frac{5^3 \times 5^4}{5^9 \times 5} =$

14) $\frac{3^3 \times 3^2}{7^2 \times 7} =$

15) $\frac{15x^5}{5x^3} =$

16) $\frac{16x^3}{4x^5} =$

17) $\frac{72y^2}{8x^3y^6} =$

18) $\frac{10x^3y^4}{50x^2y^3} =$

19) $\frac{13y^2}{52x^4y^4} =$

20) $\frac{50xy^3}{200x^3y^4} =$

21) $\frac{48x^2}{56x^2y^2} =$

22) $\frac{81y^6x}{54x^4y^3} =$

Solve.

23) $(x^3y^3)^2 =$

24) $(3x^3y^4)^3 =$

25) $(4x \times 6xy^3)^2 =$

26) $(5x \times 2y^3)^3 =$

27) $\left(\frac{9x}{x^3}\right)^2 =$

28) $(\frac{3y}{18y^2})^2 =$

29) $\left(\frac{3x^2y^3}{24x^4y^2}\right)^3 =$

30) $\left(\frac{26x^5y^3}{52x^3y^5}\right)^2 =$

31) $\left(\frac{18x^7y^4}{72x^5y^2}\right)^2 =$

32) $\left(\frac{12x^6y^4}{48x^5y^3}\right)^2 =$

Evaluate each expression. (Zero and Negative Exponents)

33) $(\frac{1}{4})^{-2} =$

34) $(\frac{1}{3})^{-2} =$

35) $(\frac{1}{7})^{-3} =$

36) $(\frac{2}{5})^{-3} =$

37) $(\frac{2}{3})^{-3} =$

38) $(\frac{3}{5})^{-4} =$

Write each expression with positive exponents.

39) $x^{-7} =$

40) $3y^{-5} =$

41) $15y^{-3} =$

42) $-20x^{-4} =$

43) $12a^{-3}b^{5} =$

44) $25a^{3}b^{-4}c^{-3} =$

45) $-4x^{5}y^{-3}z^{-6} =$

46) $\frac{18y}{x^{3}y^{-2}} =$

47) $\frac{20a^{-2}b}{-12c^{-4}}$

Write each number in scientific notation.

48) $0.00412 =$

49) $0.000053 =$

50) $66,000 =$

51) $72,000,000 =$

Evaluate.

52) $\sqrt{8} \times \sqrt{8} =$ ....

53) $\sqrt{36} - \sqrt{9} =$ ....

54) $\sqrt{81} + \sqrt{16} =$ ....

55) $\sqrt{4} \times \sqrt{25} =$ ....

56) $\sqrt{2} \times \sqrt{32} =$ ....

57) $4\sqrt{3} + 5\sqrt{3} =$ ....

Chapter 6: Answers

1) $4x^3y^2$
2) $15x^5y^3$
3) $6x^6y^5$
4) $14x^3y^4$
5) $-5x^8y^7$
6) $-24x^6y^4$
7) $-30x^6y^8$
8) $-6x^6y^5$
9) $-24x^9y^6$
10) $-10x^{10}y^5$
11) $-21x^6y^9$
12) $-18x^8y^2$
13) $\frac{1}{125}$
14) $\frac{243}{343}$
15) $3x^2$
16) $\frac{4}{x^2}$
17) $\frac{9}{x^3y^4}$
18) $\frac{xy}{5}$
19) $\frac{1}{4x^4y^2}$
20) $\frac{1}{4x^2y}$
21) $\frac{6}{7y^2}$
22) $\frac{3y^3}{2x^3}$
23) x^6y^6
24) $27x^9y^{12}$
25) $576x^4y^6$
26) $1{,}000x^3y^9$
27) $\frac{81}{x^4}$
28) $\frac{1}{36y^2}$
29) $\frac{y^3}{512x^6}$
30) $\frac{x^4}{4y^4}$
31) $\frac{x^4y^4}{16}$
32) $\frac{x^2y^2}{16}$
33) 16
34) 9
35) 343
36) $\frac{125}{8}$
37) $\frac{27}{8}$
38) $\frac{625}{81}$
39) $\frac{1}{x^7}$
40) $\frac{3}{y^5}$
41) $\frac{15}{y^3}$
42) $-\frac{20}{x^4}$
43) $\frac{12b^5}{a^3}$
44) $\frac{25a^3}{b^4c^3}$
45) $-\frac{4x^5}{y^3z^6}$
46) $\frac{18y^3}{x^3}$
47) $-\frac{5bc^4}{3a^2}$
48) 4.12×10^{-3}
49) 5.3×10^{-5}
50) 6.6×10^4
51) 7.2×10^7
52) 8
53) 3
54) 13
55) 10
56) 8
57) $9\sqrt{3}$

CHAPTER

7 Expressions and Variables

Math topics that you'll learn in this chapter:

- ☑ Simplifying Variable Expressions
- ☑ Simplifying Polynomial Expressions
- ☑ The Distributive Property
- ☑ Evaluating One Variable
- ☑ Evaluating Two Variables

Simplifying Variable Expressions

- In algebra, a variable is a letter used to stand for a number. The most common letters are $x, y, z, a, b, c, m, and\ n$.
- An algebraic expression is an expression that contains integers, variables, and math operations such as addition, subtraction, multiplication, division, etc.
- In an expression, we can combine "like" terms. (values with same variable and same power)

Examples:

Example 1. Simplify. $(4x + 2x + 4) =$

Solution: In this expression, there are three terms: $4x$, $2x$, and 4. Two terms are "like terms": $4x$ and $2x$. Combine like terms. $4x + 2x = 6x$. Then: $(4x + 2x + 4) = 6x + 4$ (***remember you cannot combine variables and numbers.***)

Example 2. Simplify. $-2x^2 - 5x + 4x^2 - 9 =$

Solution: Combine "like" terms: $-2x^2 + 4x^2 = 2x^2$.
Then: $-2x^2 - 5x + 4x^2 - 9 = 2x^2 - 5x - 9$.

Example 3. Simplify. $(-8 + 6x^2 + 3x^2 + 9x) =$

Solution: Combine like terms. Then:
$(-8 + 6x^2 + 3x^2 + 9x) = 9x^2 + 9x - 8$

Example 4. Simplify. $-10x + 6x^2 - 3x + 9x^2 =$

Solution: Combine "like" terms: $-10x - 3x = -13x$, and $6x^2 + 9x^2 = 15x^2$
Then: $-10x + 6x^2 - 3x + 9x^2 = -13x + 15x^2$. Write in standard form (biggest powers first): $-13x + 15x^2 = 15x^2 - 13x$

Simplifying Polynomial Expressions

- In mathematics, a polynomial is an expression consisting of variables and coefficients that involves only the operations of addition, subtraction, multiplication, and non–negative integer exponents of variables.

$$P(x) = a_n x^n + a_{n-1} x^{n-1} + \ldots + a_2 x^2 + a_1 x + a_0$$

- Polynomials must always be simplified as much as possible. It means you must add together any like terms. (values with same variable and same power)

Examples:

Example 1. Simplify this Polynomial Expressions. $3x^2 - 6x^3 - 2x^3 + 4x^4$

Solution: Combine "like" terms: $-6x^3 - 2x^3 = -8x^3$
Then: $3x^2 - 6x^3 - 2x^3 + 4x^4 = 3x^2 - 8x^3 + 4x^4$
Now, write the expression in standard form: $3x^2 - 8x^3 + 4x^4 = 4x^4 - 8x^3 + 3x^2$

Example 2. Simplify this expression. $(-5x^2 + 2x^3) - (3x^3 - 6x^2) =$

Solution: First, multiply $(-)$ into $(3x^3 - 6x^2)$:
$(-5x^2 + 2x^3) - (3x^3 - 6x^2) = -5x^2 + 2x^3 - 3x^3 + 6x^2$
Then combine "like" terms: $-5x^2 + 2x^3 - 3x^3 + 6x^2 = x^2 - x^3$
And write in standard form: $x^2 - x^3 = -x^3 + x^2$

Example 3. Simplify. $3x^3 - 9x^4 - 8x^2 + 12x^4 =$

Solution: Combine "like" terms: $-9x^4 + 12x^4 = 3x^4$
Then: $3x^3 - 9x^4 - 8x^2 + 12x^4 = 3x^3 + 3x^4 - 8x^2$
And write in standard form: $3x^3 + 3x^4 - 8x^2 = 3x^4 + 3x^3 - 8x^2$

The Distributive Property

- The distributive property (or the distributive property of multiplication over addition and subtraction) simplifies and solves expressions in the form of: $a(b+c)$ or $a(b-c)$
- The distributive property is multiplying a term outside the parentheses by the terms inside.
- Distributive Property rule: $a(b+c) = ab + ac$

Examples:

Example 1. Simply using the distributive property. $(-2)(x+3)$

Solution: Use Distributive Property rule: $a(b+c) = ab + ac$

$(-2)(x+3) = (-2 \times x) + (-2) \times (3) = -2x - 6$

Example 2. Simply. $(-5)(-2x-6)$

Solution: Use Distributive Property rule: $a(b+c) = ab + ac$

$(-5)(-2x-6) = (-5 \times -2x) + (-5) \times (-6) = 10x + 30$

Example 3. Simply. $(7)(2x-8) - 12x$

Solution: First, simplify $(7)(2x-8)$ using the distributive property.

Then: $(7)(2x-8) = 14x - 56$

Now combine like terms: $(7)(2x-8) - 12x = 14x - 56 - 12x$

In this expression, $14x$ and $-12x$ are "like terms" and we can combine them.

$14x - 12x = 2x$. Then: $14x - 56 - 12x = 2x - 56$

Evaluating One Variable

- To evaluate one variable expressions, find the variable and substitute a number for that variable.
- Perform the arithmetic operations.

Examples:

Example 1. Calculate this expression for $x = 2$. $8 + 2x$

Solution: First, substitute 2 for x.

Then: $8 + 2x = 8 + 2(2)$

Now, use order of operation to find the answer: $8 + 2(2) = 8 + 4 = 12$

Example 2. Evaluate this expression for $x = -1$. $4x - 8$

Solution: First, substitute -1 for x.

Then: $4x - 8 = 4(-1) - 8$

Now, use order of operation to find the answer: $4(-1) - 8 = -4 - 8 = -12$

Example 3. Find the value of this expression when $x = 4$. $(16 - 5x)$

Solution: First, substitute 4 for x,

Then: $16 - 5x = 16 - 5(4) = 16 - 20 = -4$

Example 4. Solve this expression for $x = -3$. $15 + 7x$

Solution: Substitute -3 for x.

Then: $15 + 7x = 15 + 7(-3) = 15 - 21 = -6$

Evaluating Two Variables

- To evaluate an algebraic expression, substitute a number for each variable.
- Perform the arithmetic operations to find the value of the expression.

Examples:

Example 1. Calculate this expression for $a = 2$ and $b = -1$. $(4a - 3b)$

Solution: First, substitute 2 for a, and -1 for b.

Then: $4a - 3b = 4(2) - 3(-1)$

Now, use order of operation to find the answer: $4(2) - 3(-1) = 8 + 3 = 11$

Example 2. Evaluate this expression for $x = -2$ and $y = 2$. $(3x + 6y)$

Solution: Substitute -2 for x, and 2 for y.

Then: $3x + 6y = 3(-2) + 6(2) = -6 + 12 = 6$

Example 3. Find the value of this expression $2(6a - 5b)$, when $a = -1$ and $b = 4$.

Solution: Substitute -1 for a, and 4 for b.

Then: $2(6a - 5b) = 2\big(6(-1) - 5(4)\big) = 2(-6 - 20) = 2(-26) = -52$

Example 4. Evaluate this expression. $-7x - 2y,\ x = 4,\ y = -3$

Solution: Substitute 4 for x, and -3 for y and simplify.

Then: $-7x - 2y = -7(4) - 2(-3) = -28 + 6 = -22$

Chapter 7: Practices

Simplify each expression.

1) $(3 + 4x - 1) =$
2) $(-5 - 2x + 7) =$
3) $(12x - 5x - 4) =$
4) $(-16x + 24x - 9) =$
5) $(6x + 5 - 15x) =$
6) $2 + 5x - 8x - 6 =$
7) $5x + 10 - 3x - 22 =$
8) $-5 - 3x^2 - 6 + 4x =$
9) $-6 + 9x^2 - 3 + x =$
10) $5x^2 + 3x - 10x - 3 =$
11) $4x^2 - 2x - 6x + 5 - 8 =$
12) $3x^2 - 5x - 7x + 2 - 4 =$
13) $9x^2 - x - 5x + 3 - 9 =$
14) $2x^2 - 7x - 3x^2 + 4x + 6 =$

Simplify each polynomial.

15) $5x^2 + 3x^3 - 9x^2 + 2x =$ ____________
16) $8x^4 + 2x^5 - 7x^4 + 3x^2 =$ ____________
17) $15x^3 + 11x - 5x^2 - 9x^3 =$ ____________
18) $(7x^3 - 3x^2) + (5x^2 - 13x) =$ ____________
19) $(12x^4 + 6x^3) + (x^3 - 5x^4) =$ ____________
20) $(15x^5 - 8x^3) - (4x^3 + x^2) =$ ____________
21) $(14x^4 + 7x^3) - (x^3 - 24) =$ ____________
22) $(20x^4 + 6x^3) - (-x^3 - 2x^4) =$ ____________
23) $(x^2 + 9x^3) + (-22x^2 + 6x^3) =$ ____________
24) $(4x^4 - 2x^3) + (-5x^3 - 8x^4) =$ ____________

Use the distributive property to simply each expression.

25) $2(6 + x) =$ ______

26) $5(3 - 2x) =$ ______

27) $7(1 - 5x) =$ ______

28) $(3 - 4x)7 =$ ______

29) $6(2 - 3x) =$ ______

30) $(-1)(-9 + x) =$ ______

31) $(-6)(3x - 2) =$ ______

32) $(-x + 12)(-4) =$ ______

33) $(-2)(1 - 6x) =$ ______

34) $(-5x - 3)(-8) =$ ______

Evaluate each expression using the value given.

35) $x = 4 \rightarrow 10 - x =$ ____

36) $x = 6 \rightarrow x + 8 =$ ____

37) $x = 3 \rightarrow 2x - 6 =$ ____

38) $x = 2 \rightarrow 10 - 4x =$ ____

39) $x = 7 \rightarrow 8x - 3 =$ ____

40) $x = 9 \rightarrow 20 - 2x =$ ____

41) $x = 5 \rightarrow 10x - 30 =$ ___

42) $x = -6 \rightarrow 5 - x =$ ____

43) $x = -3 \rightarrow 22 - 3x =$ ____

44) $x = -7 \rightarrow 10 - 9x =$ ____

45) $x = -10 \rightarrow 40 - 3x =$ ____

46) $x = -2 \rightarrow 20x - 5 =$ ____

47) $x = -5 \rightarrow -10x - 8 =$ ___

48) $x = -4 \rightarrow -1 - 4x =$ ___

Evaluate each expression using the values given.

49) $x = 2, y = 1 \rightarrow 2x + 7y =$ _____

50) $a = 3, b = 5 \rightarrow 3a - 5b =$ _____

51) $x = 6, y = 2 \rightarrow 3x - 2y + 8 =$ _____

52) $a = -2, b = 3 \rightarrow -5a + 2b + 6 =$ _____

53) $x = -4, y = -3 \rightarrow -4x + 10 - 8y =$ _____

Chapter 7: Answers

1) $4x + 2$
2) $-2x + 2$
3) $7x - 4$
4) $8x - 9$
5) $-9x + 5$
6) $-3x - 4$
7) $2x - 12$
8) $-3x^2 + 4x - 11$
9) $9x^2 + x - 9$
10) $5x^2 - 7x - 3$
11) $4x^2 - 8x - 3$
12) $3x^2 - 12x - 2$
13) $9x^2 - 6x - 6$
14) $-x^2 - 3x + 6$
15) $3x^3 - 4x^2 + 2x$
16) $2x^5 + x^4 + 3x^2$
17) $6x^3 - 5x^2 + 11x$
18) $7x^3 + 2x^2 - 13x$
19) $7x^4 + 7x^3$
20) $15x^5 - 12x^3 - x^2$
21) $14x^4 + 6x^3 + 24$
22) $22x^4 + 7x^3$
23) $15x^3 - 21x^2$
24) $-4x^4 - 7x^3$
25) $2x + 12$
26) $-10x + 15$
27) $-35x + 7$
28) $-28x + 21$
29) $-18x + 12$
30) $-x + 9$
31) $-18x + 12$
32) $4x - 48$
33) $12x - 2$
34) $40x + 24$
35) 6
36) 14
37) 0
38) 2
39) 53
40) 2
41) 20
42) 11
43) 31
44) 73
45) 70
46) -45
47) 42
48) 15
49) 11
50) -16
51) 22
52) 22
53) 50

CHAPTER

8 Equations and Inequalities

Math topics that you'll learn in this chapter:

- ☑ One-Step Equations
- ☑ Multi-Step Equations
- ☑ System of Equations
- ☑ Graphing Single–Variable Inequalities
- ☑ One-Step Inequalities
- ☑ Multi-Step Inequalities

One–Step Equations

- The values of two expressions on both sides of an equation are equal. Example: $ax = b$. In this equation, ax is equal to b.
- Solving an equation means finding the value of the variable.
- You only need to perform one Math operation to solve the one-step equations.
- To solve a one-step equation, find the inverse (opposite) operation is being performed.
- The inverse operations are:
  - ❖ Addition and subtraction
  - ❖ Multiplication and division

Examples:

Example 1. Solve this equation for x. $4x = 16 \rightarrow x = ?$

Solution: Here, the operation is multiplication (variable x is multiplied by 4) and its inverse operation is division. To solve this equation, divide both sides of equation by 4: $4x = 16 \rightarrow \frac{4x}{4} = \frac{16}{4} \rightarrow x = 4$

Example 2. Solve this equation. $x + 8 = 0 \rightarrow x = ?$

Solution: In this equation, 8 is added to the variable x. The inverse operation of addition is subtraction. To solve this equation, subtract 8 from both sides of the equation: $x + 8 - 8 = 0 - 8$. Then: $x + 8 - 8 = 0 - 8 \rightarrow x = -8$

Example 3. Solve this equation for x. $x - 12 = 0$

Solution: Here, the operation is subtraction and its inverse operation is addition. To solve this equation, add 12 to both sides of the equation: $x - 12 + 12 = 0 + 12 \rightarrow x = 12$

Multi–Step Equations

- To solve a multi-step equation, combine "like" terms on one side.
- Bring variables to one side by adding or subtracting.
- Simplify using the inverse of addition or subtraction.
- Simplify further by using the inverse of multiplication or division.
- Check your solution by plugging the value of the variable into the original equation.

Examples:

Example 1. Solve this equation for x. $4x + 8 = 20 - 2x$

Solution: First, bring variables to one side by adding $2x$ to both sides. Then:
$4x + 8 + 2x = 20 - 2x + 2x \rightarrow 4x + 8 + 2x = 20$.
Simplify: $6x + 8 = 20$. Now, subtract 8 from both sides of the equation:
$6x + 8 - 8 = 20 - 8 \rightarrow 6x = 12 \rightarrow$Divide both sides by 6:
$6x = 12 \rightarrow \frac{6x}{6} = \frac{12}{6} \rightarrow x = 2$
Let's check this solution by substituting the value of 2 for x in the original equation:
$x = 2 \rightarrow 4x + 8 = 20 - 2x \rightarrow 4(2) + 8 = 20 - 2(2) \rightarrow 16 = 16$
The answer $x = 2$ is correct.

Example 2. Solve this equation for x. $-5x + 4 = 24$

Solution: Subtract 4 from both sides of the equation.
$-5x + 4 = 24 \rightarrow -5x + 4 - 4 = 24 - 4 \rightarrow -5x = 20$
Divide both sides by -5, then: $-5x = 20 \rightarrow \frac{-5x}{-5} = \frac{20}{-5} \rightarrow x = -4$
Now, check the solution:
$x = -4 \rightarrow -5x + 4 = 24 \rightarrow -5(-4) + 4 = 24 \rightarrow 24 = 24$
The answer $x = -4$ is correct.

System of Equations

- A system of equations contains two equations and two variables. For example, consider the system of equations: $x - y = 1$ and $x + y = 5$
- The easiest way to solve a system of equations is using the elimination method. The elimination method uses the addition property of equality. You can add the same value to each side of an equation.
- For the first equation above, you can add $x + y$ to the left side and 5 to the right side of the first equation: $x - y + (x + y) = 1 + 5$. Now, if you simplify, you get: $x - y + (x + y) = 1 + 5 \rightarrow 2x = 6 \rightarrow x = 3$. Now, substitute 3 for the x in the first equation: $3 - y = 1$. By solving this equation, $y = 2$

Example:

What is the value of $x + y$ in this system of equations?

$$\begin{cases} 2x + 4y = 12 \\ 4x - 2y = -16 \end{cases}$$

Solution: Solving a System of Equations by Elimination:

Multiply the first equation by (-2), then add it to the second equation.

$$\begin{array}{r} -2(2x + 4y = 12) \\ \underline{4x - 2y = -16} \end{array} \Rightarrow \quad \begin{array}{r} -4x - 8y = -24 \\ 4x - 2y = -16 \end{array} \Rightarrow (-4x) + 4x - 8y - 2y = -24 - 16 \Rightarrow$$

$$-10y = -40 \Rightarrow y = 4$$

Plug in the value of y into one of the equations and solve for x.

$2x + 4(4) = 12 \Rightarrow 2x + 16 = 12 \Rightarrow 2x = -4 \Rightarrow x = -2$

Thus, $x + y = -2 + 4 = 2$

bit.ly/3mPGO6k
Find more at

Graphing Single–Variable Inequalities

- An inequality compares two expressions using an inequality sign.
- Inequality signs are: "less than" $<$, "greater than" $>$, "less than or equal to" $\leq$, and "greater than or equal to" $\geq$.
- To graph a single–variable inequality, find the value of the inequality on the number line.
- For less than ($<$) or greater than ($>$) draw an open circle on the value of the variable. If there is an equal sign too, then use a filled circle.
- Draw an arrow to the right for greater or to the left for less than.

Examples:

Example 1. Draw a graph for this inequality. $x > 2$

Solution: Since the variable is greater than 2, then we need to find 2 in the number line and draw an open circle on it. Then, draw an arrow to the right.

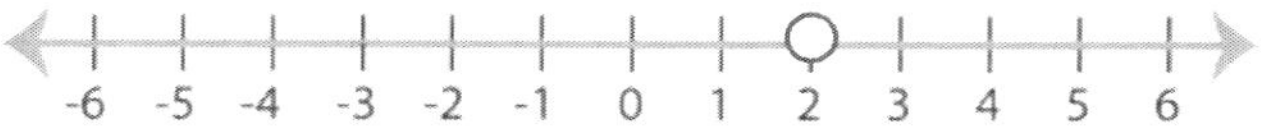

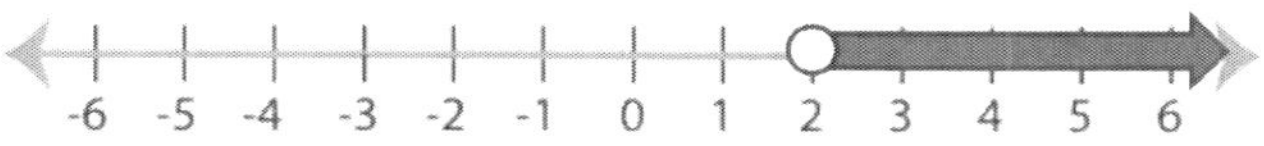

Example 2. Graph this inequality. $x \leq -3$.

Solution: Since the variable is less than or equal to -3, then we need to find -3 on the number line and draw a filled circle on it. Then, draw an arrow to the left.

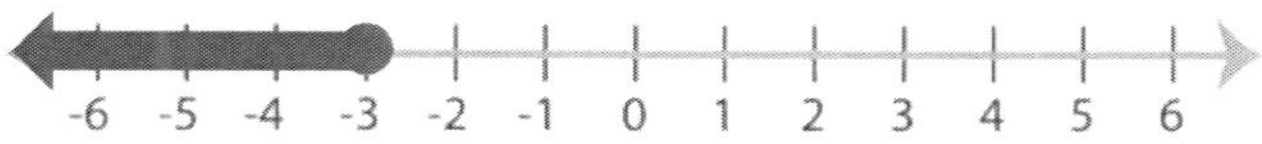

Find more at bit.ly/3aJ4GGo

One–Step Inequalities

- An inequality compares two expressions using an inequality sign.
- Inequality signs are: "less than" $<$, "greater than" $>$, "less than or equal to" $\leq$, and "greater than or equal to" $\geq$.
- You only need to perform one Math operation to solve the one-step inequalities.
- To solve one-step inequalities, find the inverse (opposite) operation is being performed.
- For dividing or multiplying both sides by negative numbers, flip the direction of the inequality sign.

Examples:

Example 1. Solve this inequality for x. $x + 5 \geq 4$

Solution: The inverse (opposite) operation of addition is subtraction. In this inequality, 5 is added to x. To isolate x we need to subtract 5 from both sides of the inequality.
Then: $x + 5 \geq 4 \rightarrow x + 5 - 5 \geq 4 - 5 \rightarrow x \geq -1$. The solution is: $x \geq -1$

Example 2. Solve the inequality. $x - 3 > -6$

Solution: 3 is subtracted from x. Add 3 to both sides.
$x - 3 > -6 \rightarrow x - 3 + 3 > -6 + 3 \rightarrow x > -3$

Example 3. Solve. $4x \leq -8$

Solution: 4 is multiplied to x. Divide both sides by 4.
Then: $4x \leq -8 \rightarrow \frac{4x}{4} \leq \frac{-8}{4} \rightarrow x \leq -2$

Example 4. Solve. $-3x \leq 6$

Solution: -3 is multiplied to x. Divide both sides by -3. Remember when dividing or multiplying both sides of an inequality by negative numbers, flip the direction of the inequality sign.
Then: $-3x \leq 6 \rightarrow \frac{-3x}{-3} \geq \frac{6}{-3} \rightarrow x \geq -2$

Multi–Step Inequalities

- To solve a multi-step inequality, combine "like" terms on one side.
- Bring variables to one side by adding or subtracting.
- Isolate the variable.
- Simplify using the inverse of addition or subtraction.
- Simplify further by using the inverse of multiplication or division.
- For dividing or multiplying both sides by negative numbers, flip the direction of the inequality sign.

Examples:

Example 1. Solve this inequality. $8x - 2 \leq 14$

Solution: In this inequality, 2 is subtracted from $8x$. The inverse of subtraction is addition. Add 2 to both sides of the inequality:
$8x - 2 + 2 \leq 14 + 2 \rightarrow 8x \leq 16$
Now, divide both sides by 8. Then: $8x \leq 16 \rightarrow \frac{8x}{8} \leq \frac{16}{8} \rightarrow x \leq 2$

The solution of this inequality is $x \leq 2$.

Example 2. Solve this inequality. $3x + 9 < 12$

Solution: First, subtract 9 from both sides: $3x + 9 - 9 < 12 - 9$
Then simplify: $3x + 9 - 9 < 12 - 9 \rightarrow 3x < 3$
Now divide both sides by 3: $\frac{3x}{3} < \frac{3}{3} \rightarrow x < 1$

Example 3. Solve this inequality. $-5x + 3 \geq 8$

Solution: First, subtract 3 from both sides:
$-5x + 3 - 3 \geq 8 - 3 \rightarrow -5x \geq 5$
Divide both sides by -5. Remember that you need to flip the direction of inequality sign. $-5x \geq 5 \rightarrow \frac{-5x}{-5} \leq \frac{5}{-5} \rightarrow x \leq -1$

Chapter 8: Practices

Solve each equation. (One–Step Equations)

1) $x + 6 = 3 \rightarrow x =$ ____

2) $5 = 11 - x \rightarrow x =$ ____

3) $-3 = 8 + x \rightarrow x =$ ____

4) $x - 2 = -7 \rightarrow x =$ ____

5) $-15 = x + 6 \rightarrow x =$ ____

6) $10 - x = -2 \rightarrow x =$ ____

7) $22 - x = -9 \rightarrow x =$ ____

8) $-4 + x = 28 \rightarrow x =$ ____

9) $11 - x = -7 \rightarrow x =$ ____

10) $35 - x = -7 \rightarrow x =$ ____

Solve each equation. (Multi–Step Equations)

11) $4(x + 2) = 12 \rightarrow x =$ ____

12) $-6(6 - x) = 12 \rightarrow x =$ ____

13) $5 = -5\,(x + 2) \rightarrow x =$ ____

14) $-10 = 2(4 + x) \rightarrow x =$ ____

15) $4(x + 2) = -12,\ x =$ ____

16) $-6(3 + 2x) = 30,\ x =$ ____

17) $-3(4 - x) = 12,\ x =$ ____

18) $-4(6 - x) = 16,\ x =$ ____

Solve each system of equations.

19) $\begin{cases} x + 6y = 32 \\ x + 3y = 17 \end{cases}$ $x =$ ____ $y =$ ____

20) $\begin{cases} 3x + y = 15 \\ x + 2y = 10 \end{cases}$ $x =$ ____ $y =$ ____

21) $\begin{cases} 3x + 5y = 17 \\ 2x + y = 9 \end{cases}$ $x =$ ____ $y =$ ____

22) $\begin{cases} 5x - 2y = -8 \\ -6x + 2y = 10 \end{cases}$ $x =$ ____ $y =$ ____

Draw a graph for each inequality.

23) $x \leq -3$

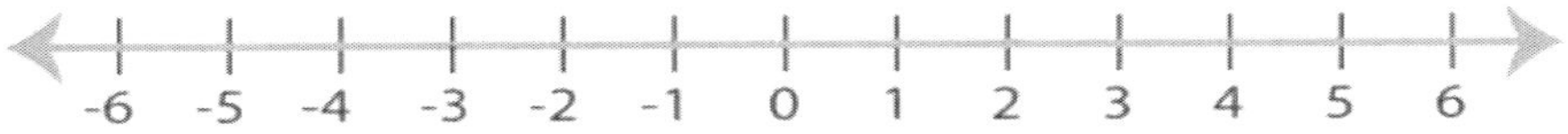

24) $x > -5$

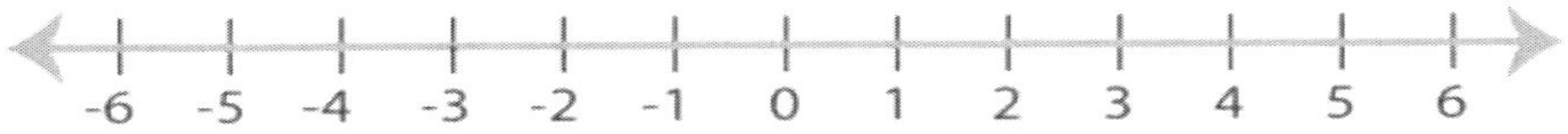

Solve each inequality and graph it.

25) $x - 2 \geq -2$

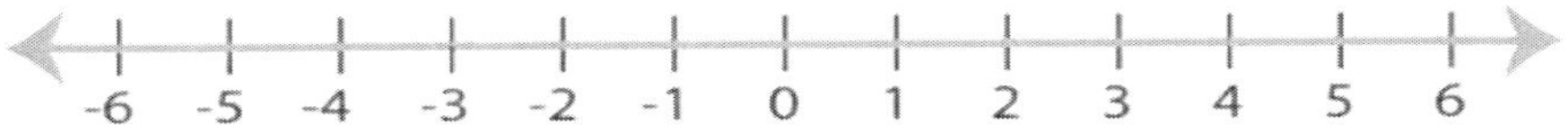

26) $2x - 3 < 9$

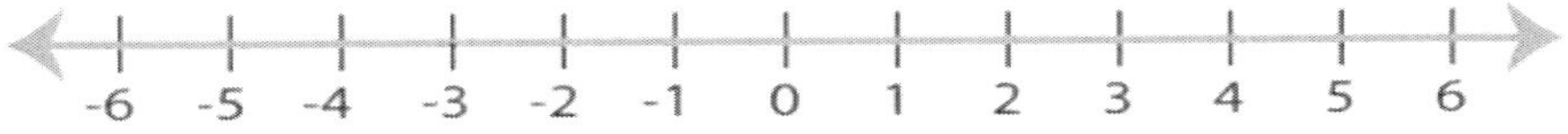

Solve each inequality.

27) $x + 13 > 4$

28) $x + 6 > 5$

29) $-12 + 2x \leq 26$

30) $-2 + 8x \leq 14$

31) $6 + 4x \leq 18$

32) $4(x + 3) \geq -12$

33) $2(6 + x) \geq -12$

34) $3(x - 5) < -6$

35) $10 + 5x < -15$

36) $6(6 + x) \geq -18$

37) $2(x - 5) \geq -14$

38) $6(x + 4) < -12$

39) $3(x - 8) \geq -48$

40) $-(6 - 4x) > -30$

41) $2(2 + 2x) > -60$

42) $-3(4 + 2x) > -24$

Chapter 8: Answers

1) -3
2) 6
3) -11
4) -5
5) -21
6) 12
7) 31
8) 32
9) 18
10) 42
11) 1
12) 8
13) -3
14) -9
15) -5
16) -4
17) 8
18) 10
19) $x = 2, y = 5$
20) $x = 4, y = 3$
21) $x = 4, y = 1$
22) $x = -2, y = -1$

23) $x \leq -3$

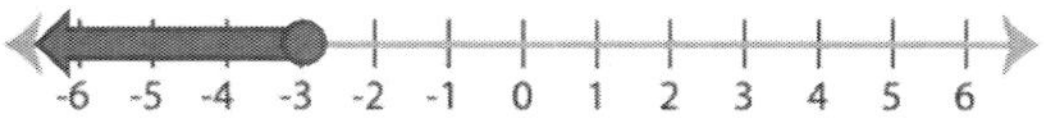

24) $x > -5$

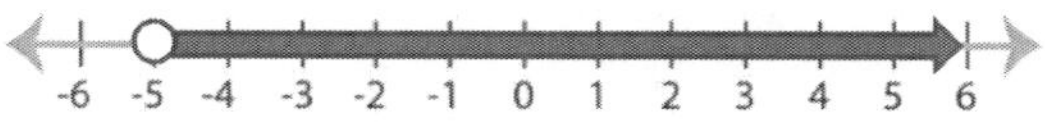

25) $x \geq 0$

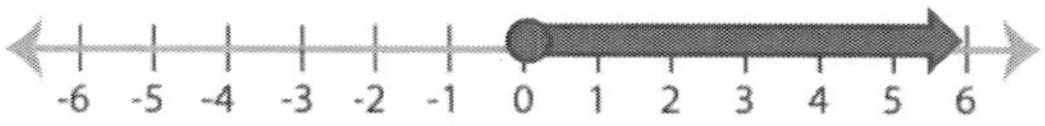

26) $x < 6$

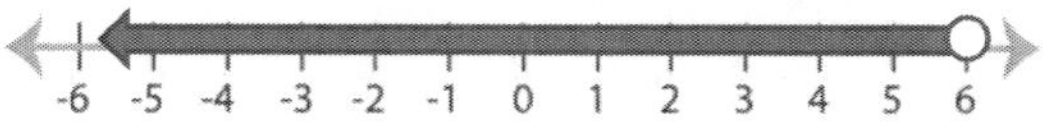

27) $x > -9$
28) $x > -1$
29) $x \leq 19$
30) $x \leq 2$
31) $x \leq 3$
32) $x \geq -6$
33) $x \geq -12$
34) $x < 3$
35) $x < -5$
36) $x \geq -9$
37) $x \geq -2$
38) $x < -6$
39) $x \geq -8$
40) $x > -6$
41) $x > -16$
42) $x < 2$

CHAPTER

9 Lines and Slope

Math topics that you'll learn in this chapter:

- ☑ Finding Slope
- ☑ Graphing Lines Using Slope–Intercept Form
- ☑ Writing Linear Equations
- ☑ Finding Midpoint
- ☑ Finding Distance of Two Points
- ☑ Graphing Linear Inequalities

Finding Slope

- The slope of a line represents the direction of a line on the coordinate plane.
- A coordinate plane contains two perpendicular number lines. The horizontal line is x and the vertical line is y. The point at which the two axes intersect is called the origin. An ordered pair (x, y) shows the location of a point.
- A line on a coordinate plane can be drawn by connecting two points.
- To find the slope of a line, we need the equation of the line or two points on the line.
- The slope of a line with two points A (x_1, y_1) and B (x_2, y_2) can be found by using this formula: $\frac{y_2 - y_1}{x_2 - x_1} = \frac{rise}{\text{run}}$
- The equation of a line is typically written as $y = mx + b$ where m is the slope and b is the y-intercept.

Examples:

Example 1. Find the slope of the line through these two points:

$A(1, -6)$ *and* $B(3, 2)$.

Solution: Slope $= \frac{y_2 - y_1}{x_2 - x_1}$. Let (x_1, y_1) be $A(1, -6)$ and (x_2, y_2) be $B(3, 2)$.

(Remember, you can choose any point for (x_1, y_1) and (x_2, y_2)).

Then: slope $= \frac{y_2 - y_1}{x_2 - x_1} = \frac{2-(-6)}{3-1} = \frac{8}{2} = 4$

The slope of the line through these two points is 4.

Example 2. Find the slope of the line with equation $y = -2x + 8$

Solution: When the equation of a line is written in the form of $y = mx + b$, the slope is m. In this line: $y = -2x + 8$, the slope is -2.

Graphing Lines Using Slope–Intercept Form

- Slope–intercept form of a line: given the slope $\boldsymbol{m}$ and the $\boldsymbol{y}$–intercept (the intersection of the line and y-axis) $\boldsymbol{b}$, then the equation of the line is:

$$\boldsymbol{y = mx + b}$$

- To draw the graph of a linear equation in a slope-intercept form on the xy coordinate plane, find two points on the line by plugging two values for x and calculating the values of y.
- You can also use the slope (m) and one point to graph the line.

Example:

Sketch the graph of $y = 2x - 4$.

Solution: To graph this line, we need to find two points. When x is zero the value of y is -4. And when x is 2 the value of y is 0.

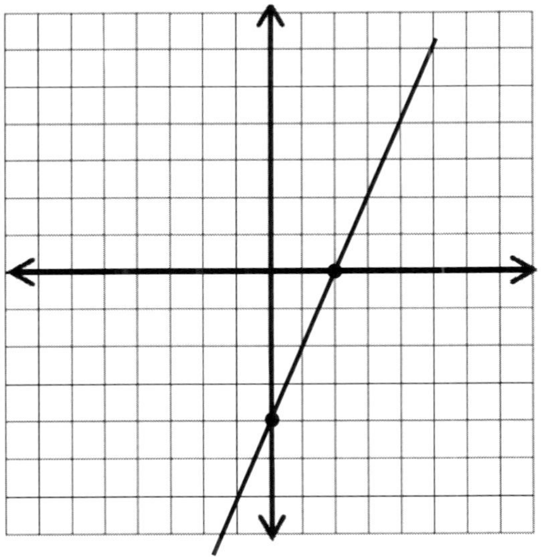

$x = 0 \rightarrow y = 2(0) - 4 = -4,$

$y = 0 \rightarrow 0 = 2x - 4 \rightarrow x = 2$

Now, we have two points:

$(0, -4)$ and $(2, 0)$.

Find the points on the coordinate plane and graph the line. Remember that the slope of the line is 2.

bit.ly/3hfdnJL

Find more at

Writing Linear Equations

- The equation of a line in slope-intercept form: $\boldsymbol{y = mx + b}$
- To write the equation of a line, first identify the slope.
- Find the y-intercept. This can be done by substituting the slope and the coordinates of a point $(\boldsymbol{x}, \boldsymbol{y})$ on the line.

Examples:

Example 1. What is the equation of the line that passes through $(3, -4)$ and has a slope of 6?

Solution: The general slope-intercept form of the equation of a line is
$y = mx + b$, where m is the slope and b is the y-intercept.
By substitution of the given point and given slope:
$y = mx + b \rightarrow -4 = (6)(3) + b$. So, $b = -4 - 18 = -22$, and the required equation of the line is: $y = 6x - 22$

Example 2. Write the equation of the line through two points $A(3,1)$ and $B(-2,6)$.

Solution: First, find the slope: $Slop = \frac{y_2 - y_1}{x_2 - x_1} = \frac{6-1}{-2-3} = \frac{5}{-5} = -1 \rightarrow m = -1$
To find the value of b, use either points and plug in the values of x and y in the equation. The answer will be the same: $y = -x + b$. Let's check both points. Then: $(3, 1) \rightarrow y = mx + b \rightarrow 1 = -1(3) + b \rightarrow b = 4$
$(-2,6) \rightarrow y = mx + b \rightarrow 6 = -1(-2) + b \rightarrow b = 4$.
The y-intercept of the line is 4. The equation of the line is: $y = -x + 4$

Example 3. What is the equation of the line that passes through $(4, -1)$ and has a slope of 4?

Solution: The general slope-intercept form of the equation of a line is
$y = mx + b$, where m is the slope and b is the y-intercept. By substitution of the given point and given slope: $y = mx + b \rightarrow -1 = (4)(4) + b$
So, $b = -1 - 16 = -17$, and the equation of the line is: $y = 4x - 17$.

Finding Midpoint

- The middle of a line segment is its midpoint.
- The Midpoint of two endpoints A (x_1, y_1) and B (x_2, y_2) can be found using this formula: M $\left(\frac{x_1+x_2}{2}, \frac{y_1+y_2}{2}\right)$

Examples:

Example 1. Find the midpoint of the line segment with the given endpoints. $(2, -4), (6, 8)$

Solution: Midpoint $= \left(\frac{x_1+x_2}{2}, \frac{y_1+y_2}{2}\right) \rightarrow (x_1, y_1) = (2, -4)$ and $(x_2, y_2) = (6, 8)$

Midpoint $= \left(\frac{2+6}{2}, \frac{-4+8}{2}\right) \rightarrow \left(\frac{8}{2}, \frac{4}{2}\right) \rightarrow M(4, 2)$

Example 2. Find the midpoint of the line segment with the given endpoints. $(-2, 3), (6, -7)$

Solution: Midpoint $= \left(\frac{x_1+x_2}{2}, \frac{y_1+y_2}{2}\right) \rightarrow (x_1, y_1) = (-2,3)$ and $(x_2, y_2) = (6, -7)$

Midpoint $= \left(\frac{-2+6}{2}, \frac{3+(-7)}{2}\right) \rightarrow \left(\frac{4}{2}, \frac{-4}{2}\right) \rightarrow M(2, -2)$

Example 3. Find the midpoint of the line segment with the given endpoints. $(7, -4), (1, 8)$

Solution: Midpoint $= \left(\frac{x_1+x_2}{2}, \frac{y_1+y_2}{2}\right) \rightarrow (x_1, y_1) = (7, -4)$ and $(x_2, y_2) = (1, 8)$

Midpoint $= \left(\frac{7+1}{2}, \frac{-4+8}{2}\right) \rightarrow \left(\frac{8}{2}, \frac{4}{2}\right) \rightarrow M(4, 2)$

Example 4. Find the midpoint of the line segment with the given endpoints. $(6, 3), (10, -9)$

Solution: Midpoint $= \left(\frac{x_1+x_2}{2}, \frac{y_1+y_2}{2}\right) \rightarrow (x_1, y_1) = (6, 3)$and $(x_2, y_2) = (10, -9)$

Midpoint $= \left(\frac{6+10}{2}, \frac{3-9}{2}\right) \rightarrow \left(\frac{16}{2}, \frac{-6}{2}\right) \rightarrow M(8, -3)$

Finding Distance of Two Points

- Use the following formula to find the distance of two points with the coordinates A (x_1, y_1) and B (x_2, y_2):

$$d = \sqrt{(x_2 - x_1)^2 + (y_2 - y_1)^2}$$

Examples:

Example 1. Find the distance between $(4, 2)$ and $(-5, -10)$ on the coordinate plane.

Solution: Use distance of two points formula: $d = \sqrt{(x_2 - x_1)^2 + (y_2 - y_1)^2}$

$(x_1, y_1) = (4, 2)$ and $(x_2, y_2) = (-5, -10)$. Then: $d = \sqrt{(x_2 - x_1)^2 + (y_2 - y_1)^2} \rightarrow$

$$= \sqrt{(-5 - 4)^2 + (-10 - 2)^2} = \sqrt{(-9)^2 + (-12)^2} = \sqrt{81 + 144} = \sqrt{225} = 15$$

Then: $d = 15$

Example 2. Find the distance of two points $(-1, 5)$ and $(-4, 1)$.

Solution: Use distance of two points formula: $d = \sqrt{(x_2 - x_1)^2 + (y_2 - y_1)^2}$

$(x_1, y_1) = (-1, 5)$, and $(x_2, y_2) = (-4, 1)$

Then: $= \sqrt{(x_2 - x_1)^2 + (y_2 - y_1)^2} \rightarrow d = \sqrt{(-4 - (-1))^2 + (1 - 5)^2} =$

$\sqrt{(-3)^2 + (-4)^2} = \sqrt{9 + 16} = \sqrt{25} = 5$. Then: $d = 5$

Example 3. Find the distance between $(-6, 5)$ and $(-1, -7)$.

Solution: Use distance of two points formula: $d = \sqrt{(x_2 - x_1)^2 + (y_2 - y_1)^2}$

$(x_1, y_1) = (-6, 5)$ and $(x_2, y_2) = (-1, -7)$. Then: $d = \sqrt{(x_2 - x_1)^2 + (y_2 - y_1)^2}$

$$d = \sqrt{\left(-1 - (-6)\right)^2 + (-7 - 5)^2} = \sqrt{(5)^2 + (-12)^2} = \sqrt{25 + 144} = \sqrt{169}$$

$$= 13$$

Graphing Linear Inequalities

- To graph a linear inequality, first draw a graph of the "equals" line.
- Use a dash line for less than (<) and greater than (>) signs and a solid line for less than and equal to (≤) and greater than and equal to (≥).
- Choose a testing point. (it can be any point on both sides of the line.)
- Put the value of (x, y) of that point in the inequality. If that works, that part of the line is the solution. If the values don't work, then the other part of the line is the solution.

Example:

Sketch the graph of inequality: $y < 2x + 4$

Solution: To draw the graph of $y < 2x + 4$, you first need to graph the line:

$y = 2x + 4$

Since there is a less than (<) sign, draw a dash line.

The slope is 2 and y-intercept is 4.

Then, choose a testing point and substitute the value of x and y from that point into the inequality. The easiest point to test is the origin: $(0, 0)$

$$(0, 0) \rightarrow y < 2x + 4 \rightarrow 0 < 2(0) + 4 \rightarrow 0 < 4$$

This is correct! 0 is less than 4. So, this part of the line (on the right side) is the solution of this inequality.

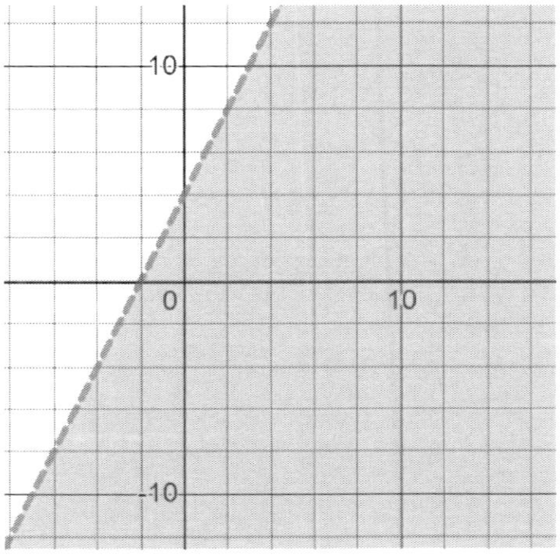

Chapter 9: Practices

Find the slope of each line.

1) $y = x - 5$
2) $y = 2x + 6$
3) $y = -5x - 8$
4) Line through $(2, 6)$ *and* $(5, 0)$
5) Line through $(8, 0)$ *and* $(-4, 3)$
6) Line through $(-2, -4)$ *and* $(-4, 8)$

Sketch the graph of each line. (Using Slope–Intercept Form)

7) $y = x + 4$

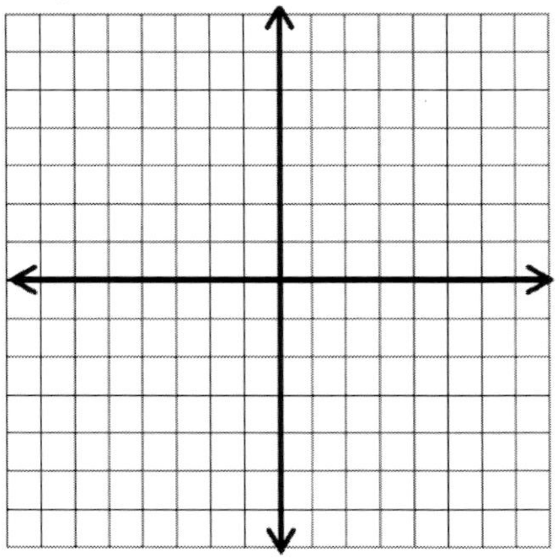

8) $y = 2x - 5$

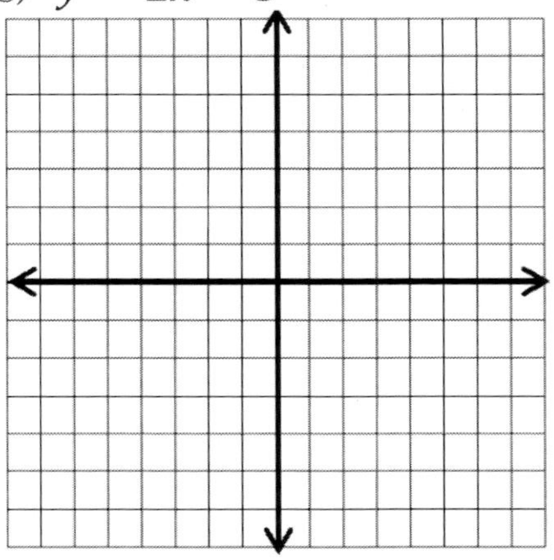

Solve.

9) What is the equation of a line with slope 4 and intercept 16? ______________

10) What is the equation of a line with slope 3 and passes through point $(1, 5)$? ______________

11) What is the equation of a line with slope -5 and passes through point $(-2, 7)$? ______________

12) The slope of a line is -4 and it passes through point $(-6, 2)$. What is the equation of the line? ______________

13) The slope of a line is -3 and it passes through point $(-3, -6)$. What is the equation of the line? ______________

Sketch the graph of each linear inequality.

14) $y > 2x - 2$

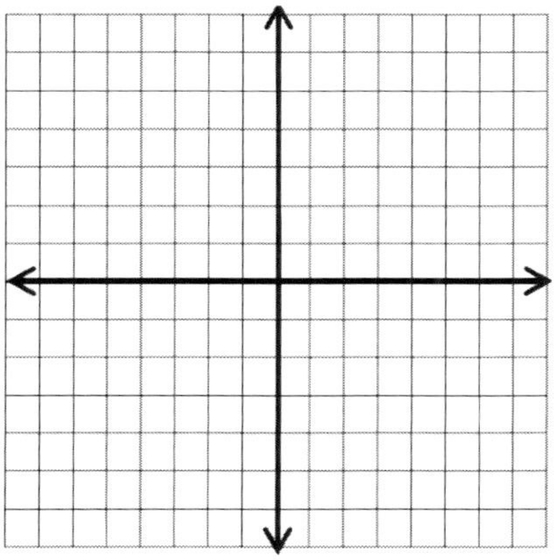

15) $y < -x + 3$

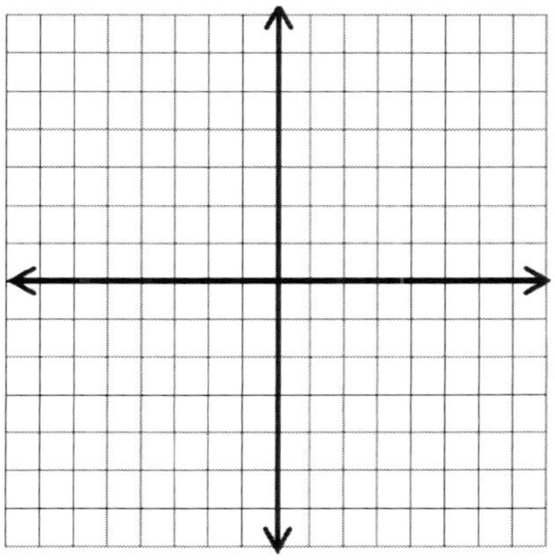

Find the midpoint of the line segment with the given endpoints.

16) $(5, 0), (1, 4)$

17) $(2, 3), (4, 7)$

18) $(8, 1), (2, 5)$

19) $(5, 10), (3, 6)$

20) $(4, -1), (-2, 7)$

21) $(2, -5), (4, 1)$

22) $(7, 6), (-5, 2)$

23) $(-2, 8), (4, -6)$

Find the distance between each pair of points.

24) $(-2, 8), (-6, 8)$

25) $(4, -4), (14, 20)$

26) $(-1, 9), (-5, 6)$

27) $(0, 3), (4, 3)$

28) $(0, -2), (5, 10)$

29) $(4, 3), (7, -1)$

30) $(2, 6), (10, -9)$

31) $(3, 3), (6, -1)$

32) $(-2, -12), (14, 18)$

33) $(2, -2), (12, 22)$

Chapter 9: Answers

1) 1
2) 2
3) -5
4) -2
5) $-\frac{1}{4}$
6) -6

7) $y = x + 4$

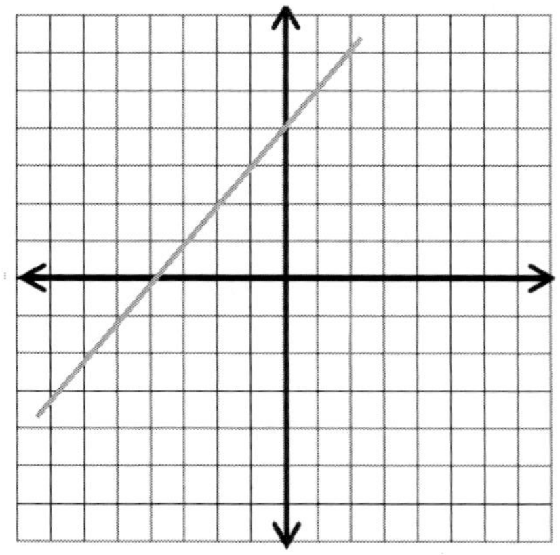

8) $y = 2x - 5$

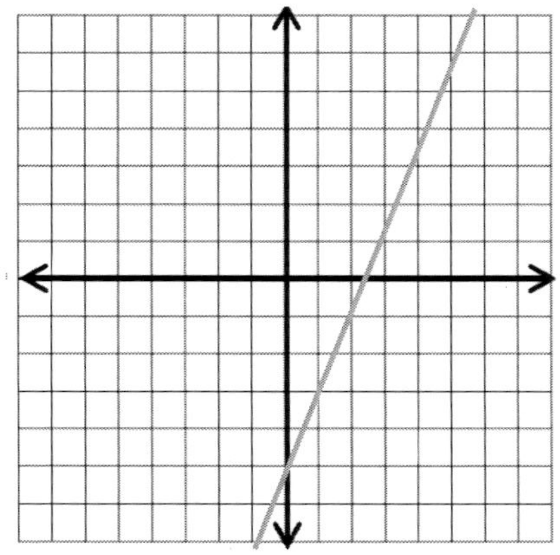

9) $y = 4x + 16$
10) $y = 3x + 2$
11) $y = -5x - 3$
12) $y = -4x - 22$
13) $y = -3x - 15$

14) $y > 2x - 2$

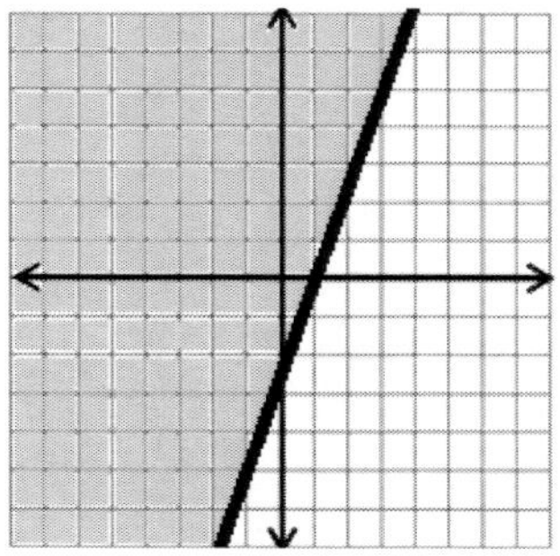

15) $y < -x + 3$

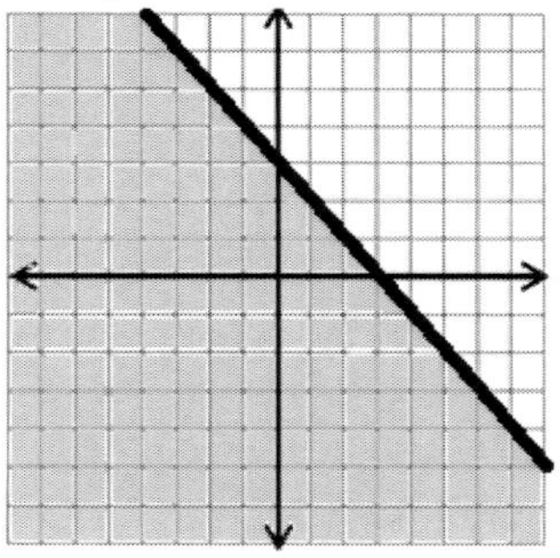

16) $(3,2)$
17) $(3,5)$
18) $(5,3)$
19) $(4,8)$
20) $(1,3)$
21) $(3,-2)$
22) $(1,4)$
23) $(1,1)$
24) 4
25) 26
26) 5
27) 4
28) 13
29) 5
30) 17
31) 5
32) 34
33) 26

CHAPTER

10 Polynomials

Math topics that you'll learn in this chapter:

- ☑ Simplifying Polynomials
- ☑ Adding and Subtracting Polynomials
- ☑ Multiplying Monomials
- ☑ Multiplying and Dividing Monomials
- ☑ Multiplying a Polynomial and a Monomial
- ☑ Multiplying Binomials
- ☑ Factoring Trinomials

Simplifying Polynomials

- To simplify Polynomials, find "like" terms. (they have same variables with same power).
- Use "FOIL". (First–Out–In–Last) for binomials:

$$(x+a)(x+b) = x^2 + (b+a)x + ab$$

- Add or Subtract "like" terms using order of operation.

Examples:

Example 1. Simplify this expression. $x(4x+7) - 2x =$

Solution: Use Distributive Property: $x(4x+7) = 4x^2 + 7x$

Now, combine like terms: $x(4x+7) - 2x = 4x^2 + 7x - 2x = 4x^2 + 5x$

Example 2. Simplify this expression. $(x+3)(x+5) =$

Solution: First, apply the FOIL method: $(a+b)(c+d) = ac + ad + bc + bd$

$(x+3)(x+5) = x^2 + 5x + 3x + 15$

Now combine like terms: $x^2 + 5x + 3x + 15 = x^2 + 8x + 15$

Example 3. Simplify this expression. $2x(x-5) - 3x^2 + 6x =$

Solution: Use Distributive Property: $2x(x-5) = 2x^2 - 10x$

Then: $2x(x-5) - 3x^2 + 6x = 2x^2 - 10x - 3x^2 + 6x$

Now combine like terms: $2x^2 - 3x^2 = -x^2$, and $-10x + 6x = -4x$

The simplified form of the expression: $2x^2 - 10x - 3x^2 + 6 = -x^2 - 4x$

Adding and Subtracting Polynomials

- Adding polynomials is just a matter of combining like terms, with some order of operations considerations thrown in.
- Be careful with the minus signs, and don't confuse addition and multiplication!
- For subtracting polynomials, sometimes you need to use the Distributive Property: $a(b+c) = ab + ac$, $a(b-c) = ab - ac$

Examples:

Example 1. Simplify the expressions. $(x^2 - 2x^3) - (x^3 - 3x^2) =$

Solution: First, use Distributive Property:
$-(x^3 - 3x^2) = -x^3 + 3x^2$
$\rightarrow (x^2 - 2x^3) - (x^3 - 3x^2) = x^2 - 2x^3 - x^3 + 3x^2$
Now combine like terms: $-2x^3 - x^3 = -3x^3$ and $x^2 + 3x^2 = 4x^2$
Then: $(x^2 - 2x^3) - (x^3 - 3x^2) = x^2 - 2x^3 - x^3 + 3x^2 = -3x^3 + 4x^2$

Example 2. Add expressions. $(3x^3 - 5) + (4x^3 - 2x^2) =$

Solution: Remove parentheses:

$$(3x^3 - 5) + (4x^3 - 2x^2) = 3x^3 - 5 + 4x^3 - 2x^2$$

Now combine like terms: $3x^3 - 5 + 4x^3 - 2x^2 = 7x^3 - 2x^2 - 5$

Example 3. Simplify the expressions. $(-4x^2 - 2x^3) - (5x^2 + 2x^3) =$

Solution: First, use Distributive Property: $-(5x^2 + 2x^3) = -5x^2 - 2x^3 \rightarrow$

$$(-4x^2 - 2x^3) - (5x^2 + 2x^3) = -4x^2 - 2x^3 - 5x^2 - 2x^3$$

Now combine like terms and write in standard form:
$-4x^2 - 2x^3 - 5x^2 - 2x^3 = -4x^3 - 9x^2$

Multiplying Monomials

- A monomial is a polynomial with just one term: Examples: $2x$ or $7y^2$.
- When you multiply monomials, first multiply the coefficients (a number placed before and multiplying the variable) and then multiply the variables using multiplication property of exponents.

$$x^a \times x^b = x^{a+b}$$

Examples:

Example 1. Multiply expressions. $2xy^3 \times 6x^4y^2$

Solution: Find the same variables and use multiplication property of exponents:
$x^a \times x^b = x^{a+b}$
$x \times x^4 = x^{1+4} = x^5$ and $y^3 \times y^2 = y^{3+2} = y^5$
Then, multiply coefficients and variables: $2xy^3 \times 6x^4y^2 = 12x^5y^5$

Example 2. Multiply expressions. $7a^3b^8 \times 3a^6b^4 =$

Solution: Use the multiplication property of exponents: $x^a \times x^b = x^{a+b}$
$a^3 \times a^6 = a^{3+6} = a^9$ and $b^8 \times b^4 = b^{8+4} = b^{12}$
Then: $7a^3b^8 \times 3a^6b^4 = 21a^9b^{12}$

Example 3. Multiply. $5x^2y^4z^3 \times 4x^4y^7z^5$

Solution: Use the multiplication property of exponents: $x^a \times x^b = x^{a+b}$
$x^2 \times x^4 = x^{2+4} = x^6$, $y^4 \times y^7 = y^{4+7} = y^{11}$ and $z^3 \times z^5 = z^{3+5} = z^8$
Then: $5x^2y^4z^3 \times 4x^4y^7z^5 = 20x^6y^{11}z^8$

Example 4. Simplify. $(-6a^7b^4)(4a^8b^5) =$

Solution: Use the multiplication property of exponents: $x^a \times x^b = x^{a+b}$
$a^7 \times a^8 = a^{7+8} = a^{15}$ and $b^4 \times b^5 = b^{4+5} = b^9$
Then: $(-6a^7b^4)(4a^8b^5) = -24a^{15}b^9$

Multiplying and Dividing Monomials

- When you divide or multiply two monomials, you need to divide or multiply their coefficients and then divide or multiply their variables.
- In case of exponents with the same base, for Division, subtract their powers, for Multiplication, add their powers.
- Exponent's Multiplication and Division rules:

$$x^a \times x^b = x^{a+b}, \qquad \frac{x^a}{x^b} = x^{a-b}$$

Examples:

Example 1. Multiply expressions. $(3x^5)(9x^4) =$

Solution: Use multiplication property of exponents:
$x^a \times x^b = x^{a+b} \rightarrow x^5 \times x^4 = x^9$
Then: $(3x^5)(9x^4) = 27x^9$

Example 2. Divide expressions. $\frac{12x^4y^6}{6xy^2} =$

Solution: Use division property of exponents:
$\frac{x^a}{x^b} = x^{a-b} \rightarrow \frac{x^4}{x} = x^{4-1} = x^3$ and $\frac{y^6}{y^2} = y^{6-2} = y^4$
Then: $\frac{12x^4y^6}{6xy^2} = 2x^3y^4$

Example 3. Divide expressions. $\frac{49a^6b^9}{7a^3b^4}$

Solution: Use division property of exponents:
$\frac{x^a}{x^b} = x^{a-b} \rightarrow \frac{a^6}{a^3} = a^{6-3} = a^3$ and $\frac{b^9}{b^4} = b^{9-4} = b^5$
Then: $\frac{49a^6b^9}{7a^3b^4} = 7a^3b^5$

Multiplying a Polynomial and a Monomial

- When multiplying monomials, use the product rule for exponents.

$$x^a \times x^b = x^{a+b}$$

- When multiplying a monomial by a polynomial, use the distributive property.

$$a \times (b + c) = a \times b + a \times c = ab + ac$$
$$a \times (b - c) = a \times b - a \times c = ab - ac$$

Examples:

Example 1. Multiply expressions. $6x(2x + 5)$

Solution: Use Distributive Property:

$6x(2x + 5) = 6x \times 2x + 6x \times 5 = 12x^2 + 30x$

Example 2. Multiply expressions. $x(3x^2 + 4y^2)$

Solution: Use Distributive Property:

$x(3x^2 + 4y^2) = x \times 3x^2 + x \times 4y^2 = 3x^3 + 4xy^2$

Example 3. Multiply. $-x(-2x^2 + 4x + 5)$

Solution: Use Distributive Property:

$-x(-2x^2 + 4x + 5) = (-x)(-2x^2) + (-x) \times (4x) + (-x) \times (5) =$

Now simplify:

$(-x)(-2x^2) + (-x) \times (4x) + (-x) \times (5) = 2x^3 - 4x^2 - 5x$

Multiplying Binomials

- A binomial is a polynomial that is the sum or the difference of two terms, each of which is a monomial.
- To multiply two binomials, use the "FOIL" method. (First–Out–In–Last)

  $(x + a)(x + b) = x \times x + x \times b + a \times x + a \times b = x^2 + bx + ax + ab$

Examples:

Example 1. Multiply Binomials. $(x + 3)(x - 2) =$

Solution: Use "FOIL". (First–Out–In–Last):

$(x + 3)(x - 2) = x^2 - 2x + 3x - 6$

Then combine like terms: $x^2 - 2x + 3x - 6 = x^2 + x - 6$

Example 2. Multiply. $(x + 6)(x + 4) =$

Solution: Use "FOIL". (First–Out–In–Last):

$(x + 6)(x + 4) = x^2 + 4x + 6x + 24$

Then simplify: $x^2 + 4x + 6x + 24 = x^2 + 10x + 24$

Example 3. Multiply. $(x + 5)(x - 7) =$

Solution: Use "FOIL". (First–Out–In–Last):

$(x + 5)(x - 7) = x^2 - 7x + 5x - 35$

Then simplify: $x^2 - 7x + 5x - 35 = x^2 - 2x - 35$

Example 4. Multiply Binomials. $(x - 9)(x - 5) =$

Solution: Use "FOIL". (First–Out–In–Last):

$(x - 9)(x - 5) = x^2 - 5x - 9x + 45$

Then combine like terms: $x^2 - 5x - 9x + 45 = x^2 - 14x + 45$

Factoring Trinomials

To factor trinomials, you can use following methods:

- "FOIL": $(x+a)(x+b) = x^2 + (b+a)x + ab$
- "Difference of Squares":

$$a^2 - b^2 = (a+b)(a-b)$$
$$a^2 + 2ab + b^2 = (a+b)(a+b)$$
$$a^2 - 2ab + b^2 = (a-b)(a-b)$$

- "Reverse FOIL": $x^2 + (b+a)x + ab = (x+a)(x+b)$

Examples:

Example 1. Factor this trinomial. $x^2 - 2x - 8$

Solution: Break the expression into groups. You need to find two numbers that their product is -8 and their sum is -2. (remember "Reverse FOIL": $x^2 + (b+a)x + ab = (x+a)(x+b)$). Those two numbers are 2 and -4. Then:

$$x^2 - 2x - 8 = (x^2 + 2x) + (-4x - 8)$$

Now factor out x from $x^2 + 2x$: $x(x+2)$, and factor out -4 from $-4x - 8$: $-4(x+2)$; Then: $(x^2 + 2x) + (-4x - 8) = x(x+2) - 4(x+2)$

Now factor out like term: $(x+2)$. Then: $(x+2)(x-4)$

Example 2. Factor this trinomial. $x^2 - 2x - 24$

Solution: Break the expression into groups: $(x^2 + 4x) + (-6x - 24)$

Now factor out x from $x^2 + 4x$: $x(x+4)$, and factor out -6 from $-6x - 24$: $-6(x+4)$; Then: $(x+4) - 6(x+4)$, now factor out like term: $(x = 4) \rightarrow x(x+4) - 6(x+4) = (x+4)(x-6)$

Chapter 10: Practices

Simplify each polynomial.

1) $3(6x+4)=$

2) $5(3x-8)=$

3) $x(7x+2)+9x=$

4) $6x(x+3)+5x=$

5) $6x(3x+1)-5x=$

6) $x(3x-4)+3x^2-6=$

7) $x^2-5-3x(x+8)=$

8) $2x^2+7-6x(2x+5)=$

Add or subtract polynomials.

9) $(x^2+3)+(2x^2-4)=$

10) $(3x^2-6x)-(x^2+8x)=$

11) $(4x^3-3x^2)+(2x^3-5x^2)=$

12) $(6x^3-7x)-(5x^3-3x)=$

13) $(10x^3+4x^2)+(14x^2-8)=$

14) $(4x^3-9)-(3x^3-7x^2)=$

15) $(9x^3+3x)-(6x^3-4x)=$

16) $(7x^3-5x)-(3x^3+5x)=$

Find the products. (Multiplying Monomials)

17) $3x^2\times 8x^3=$

18) $2x^4\times 9x^3=$

19) $-4a^4b\times 2ab^3=$

20) $(-7x^3yz)\times(3xy^2z^4)=$

21) $-2a^5bc\times 6a^2b^4=$

22) $9u^3t^2\times(-2ut)=$

23) $12x^2z\times 3xy^3=$

24) $11x^3z\times 5xy^5=$

25) $-6a^3bc\times 5a^4b^3=$

26) $-4x^6y^2\times(-12xy)=$

Simplify each expression. (Multiplying and Dividing Monomials)

27) $(7x^2y^3)(3x^4y^2) =$

28) $(6x^3y^2)(4x^4y^3) =$

29) $(10x^8y^5)(3x^5y^7) =$

30) $(15a^3b^2)(2a^3b^8) =$

31) $\frac{42x^4y^2}{6x^3y} =$

32) $\frac{49x^5y^6}{7x^2y} =$

33) $\frac{63x^{15}y^{10}}{9x^8y^6} =$

34) $\frac{35x^8y^{12}}{5x^4y^8} =$

Find each product. (Multiplying a Polynomial and a Monomial)

35) $3x(5x - y) =$

36) $2x(4x + y) =$

37) $7x(x - 3y) =$

38) $x(2x^2 + 2x - 4) =$

39) $5x(3x^2 + 8x + 2) =$

40) $7x(2x^2 - 9x - 5) =$

Find each product. (Multiplying Binomials)

41) $(x - 3)(x + 3) =$

42) $(x - 6)(x + 6) =$

43) $(x + 10)(x + 4) =$

44) $(x - 6)(x + 7) =$

45) $(x + 2)(x - 5) =$

46) $(x - 10)(x + 3) =$

Factor each trinomial.

47) $x^2 + 6x + 8 =$

48) $x^2 + 3x - 10 =$

49) $x^2 + 2x - 48 =$

50) $x^2 - 10x + 16 =$

51) $2x^2 - 10x + 12 =$

52) $3x^2 - 10x + 3 =$

Chapter 10: Answers

1) $18x + 12$
2) $15x - 40$
3) $7x^2 + 11x$
4) $6x^2 + 23x$
5) $18x^2 + x$
6) $6x^2 - 4x - 6$
7) $-2x^2 - 24x - 5$
8) $-10x^2 - 30x + 7$
9) $3x^2 - 1$
10) $2x^2 - 14x$
11) $6x^3 - 8x^2$
12) $x^3 - 4x$
13) $10x^3 + 18x^2 - 8$
14) $x^3 + 7x^2 - 9$
15) $3x^3 + 7x$
16) $4x^3 - 10x$
17) $24x^5$
18) $18x^7$
19) $-8a^5b^4$
20) $-21x^4y^3z^5$
21) $-12a^7b^5c$
22) $-18u^4t^3$
23) $36x^3y^3z$
24) $55x^4y^5z$
25) $-30a^7b^4c$
26) $48x^7y^3$
27) $21x^6y^5$
28) $24x^7y^5$
29) $30x^{13}y^{12}$
30) $30a^6b^{10}$
31) $7xy$
32) $7x^3y^5$
33) $7x^7y^4$
34) $7x^4y^4$
35) $15x^2 - 3xy$
36) $8x^2 + 2xy$
37) $7x^2 - 21xy$
38) $2x^3 + 2x^2 - 4x$
39) $15x^3 + 40x^2 + 10x$
40) $14x^3 - 63x^2 - 35x$
41) $x^2 - 9$
42) $x^2 - 36$
43) $x^2 + 14x + 40$
44) $x^2 + x - 42$
45) $x^2 - 3x - 10$
46) $x^2 - 7x - 30$
47) $(x + 4)(x + 2)$
48) $(x + 5)(x - 2)$
49) $(x - 6)(x + 8)$
50) $(x - 8)(x - 2)$
51) $(2x - 4)(x - 3)$
52) $(3x - 1)(x - 3)$

CHAPTER

11 Geometry and Solid Figures

Math topics that you'll learn in this chapter:

- ☑ The Pythagorean Theorem
- ☑ Complementary and Supplementary angles
- ☑ Parallel lines and Transversals
- ☑ Triangles
- ☑ Special Right Triangles
- ☑ Polygons
- ☑ Circles
- ☑ Trapezoids
- ☑ Cubes
- ☑ Rectangle Prisms
- ☑ Cylinder

The Pythagorean Theorem

- You can use the Pythagorean Theorem to find a missing side in a right triangle.
- In any right triangle: $a^2 + b^2 = c^2$

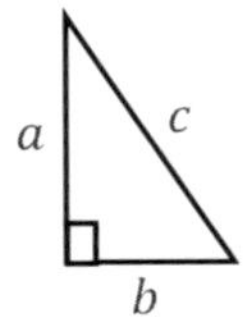

Examples:

Example 1. Right triangle ABC (not shown) has two legs of lengths 3 cm (AB) and 4 cm (AC). What is the length of the hypotenuse of the triangle (side BC)?

Solution: Use Pythagorean Theorem: $a^2 + b^2 = c^2$, $a = 3$, and $b = 4$

Then: $a^2 + b^2 = c^2 \rightarrow 3^2 + 4^2 = c^2 \rightarrow 9 + 16 = c^2 \rightarrow 25 = c^2 \rightarrow c = \sqrt{25} = 5$

The length of the hypotenuse is 5 cm.

Example 2. Find the hypotenuse of this triangle.

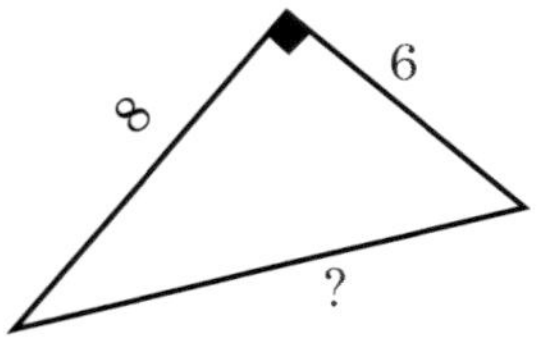

Solution: Use Pythagorean Theorem: $a^2 + b^2 = c^2$

Then: $a^2 + b^2 = c^2 \rightarrow 8^2 + 6^2 = c^2 \rightarrow 64 + 36 = c^2$

$c^2 = 100 \rightarrow c = \sqrt{100} = 10$

Example 3. Find the length of the missing side in this triangle.

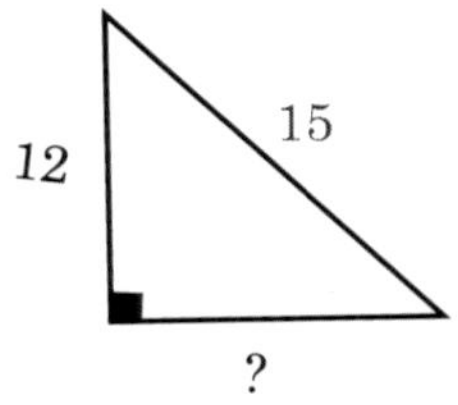

Solution: Use Pythagorean Theorem: $a^2 + b^2 = c^2$

Then: $a^2 + b^2 = c^2 \rightarrow 12^2 + b^2 = 15^2 \rightarrow 144 + b^2 = 225 \rightarrow$

$b^2 = 225 - 144 \rightarrow b^2 = 81 \rightarrow b = \sqrt{81} = 9$

Complementary and Supplementary angles

- Two angles with a sum of 90 degrees are called complementary angles.

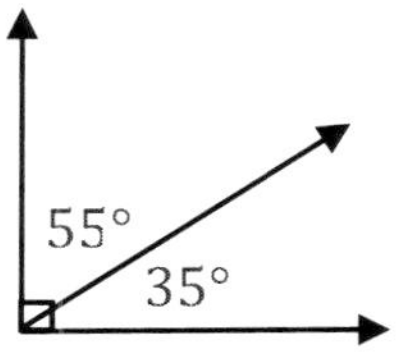

- Two angles with a sum of 180 degrees are Supplementary angles.

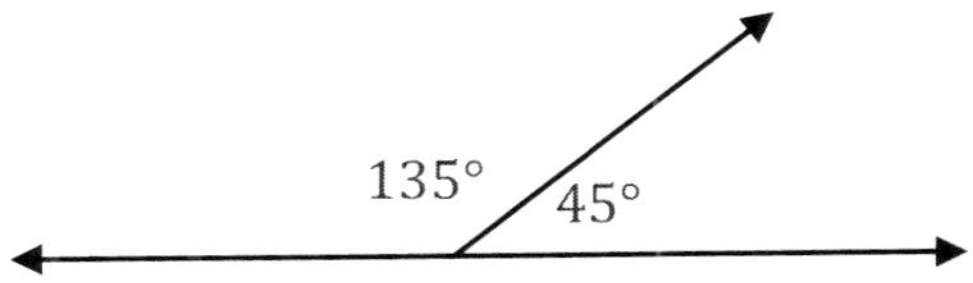

Examples:

Example 1. Find the missing angle.

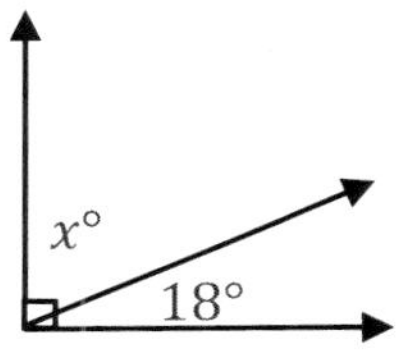

Solution: Notice that the two angles form a right angle. This means that the angles are complementary, and their sum is 90.
Then: $18 + x = 90 \rightarrow x = 90^{\circ} - 18^{\circ} = 72^{\circ}$
The missing angle is 72 degrees. $x = 72°$

Example 2. Angles Q and S are supplementary. What is the measure of angle Q if angle S is 35 degrees?

Solution: Q and S are supplementary $\rightarrow Q + S = 180 \rightarrow Q + 35 = 180 \rightarrow$

$$Q = 180 - 35 = 145$$

Example 3. Angles x and y are complementary. What is the measure of angle x if angle y is 16 degrees?

Solution: Angles x and y are complementary $\rightarrow x + y = 90 \rightarrow x + 16 = 90 \rightarrow$

$$x = 90 - 16 = 74$$

bit.ly/3nlOn6G
Find more at

Parallel lines and Transversals

- When a line (transversal) intersects two parallel lines in the same plane, eight angles are formed. In the following diagram, a transversal intersects two parallel lines. Angles 1, 3, 5, and 7 are congruent. Angles 2, 4, 6, and 8 are also congruent.
- In the following diagram, the following angles are supplementary angles (their sum is 180):

  - Angles 1 and 8
  - Angles 2 and 7
  - Angles 3 and 6
  - Angles 4 and 5

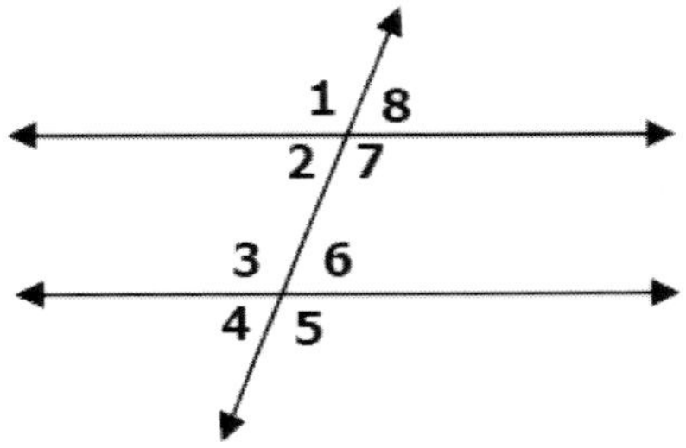

Example:

In the following diagram, two parallel lines are cut by a transversal. What is the value of x?

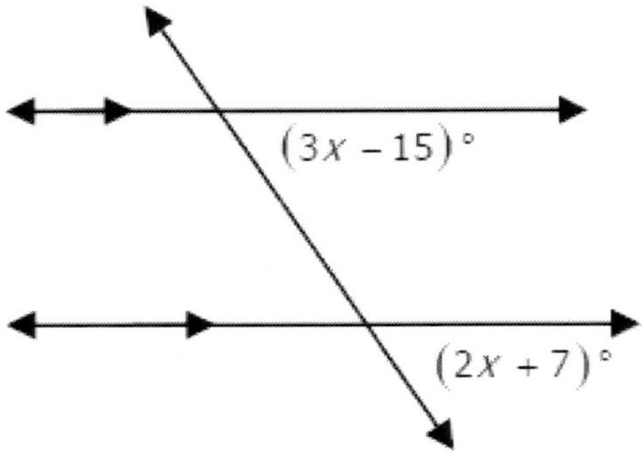

Solution: The two angles $3x - 15$ and $2x + 7$ are equivalent.

That is: $3x - 15 = 2x + 7$

Now, solve for x:

$3x - 15 + 15 = 2x + 7 + 15$

$\rightarrow 3x = 2x + 22 \rightarrow 3x - 2x = 2x + 22 - 2x \rightarrow$

$x = 22$

Find more at bit.ly/32Mcwu

Triangles

- In any triangle, the sum of all angles is 180 degrees.
- Area of a triangle $= \frac{1}{2}$ $(base \times height)$

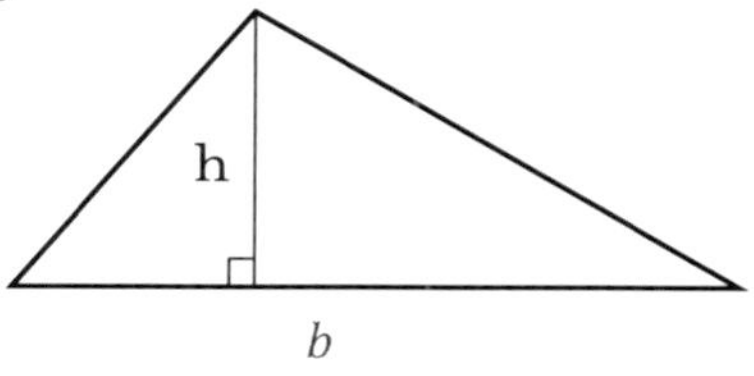

Examples:

Example 1. What is the area of this triangles?

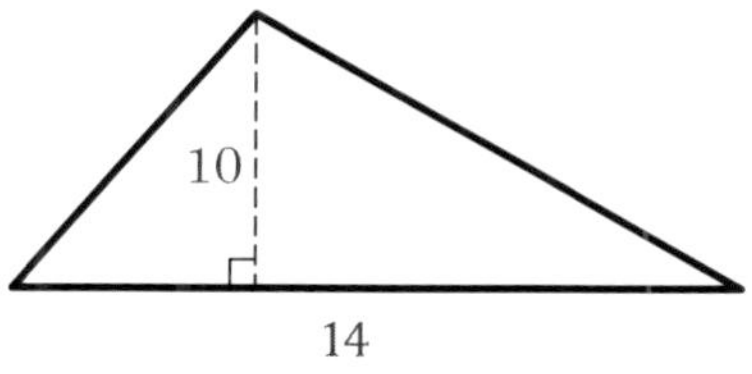

Solution: Use the area formula:

Area $= \frac{1}{2}(base \times height)$

$base = 14$ and $height = 10$, Then:

Area $= \frac{1}{2}(14 \times 10) = \frac{1}{2}(140) = 70$

Example 2. What is the area of this triangles?

Solution: Use the area formula:

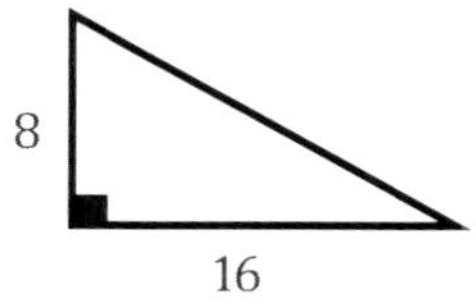

Area $= \frac{1}{2}(base \times height)$

$base = 16$ and $height = 8$; Area $= \frac{1}{2}(16 \times 8) = \frac{128}{2} = 64$

Example 3. What is the missing angle in this triangle?

Solution:

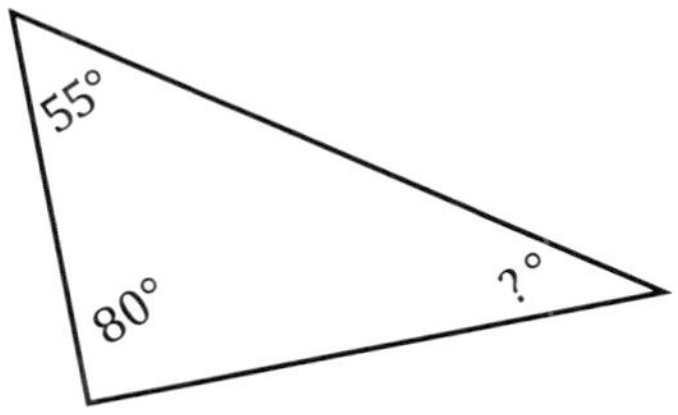

In any triangle, the sum of all angles is 180 degrees.

Let x be the missing angle.

Then: $55 + 80 + x = 180 \rightarrow 135 + x = 180 \rightarrow$

$$x = 180 - 135 = 45$$

The missing angle is 45 degrees.

bit.ly/3haZrRg
Find more at

Special Right Triangles

- A special right triangle is a triangle whose sides are in a particular ratio. Two special right triangles are $45^\circ - 45^\circ - 90^\circ$ and $30^\circ - 60^\circ - 90^\circ$ triangles.
- In a special $45^\circ - 45^\circ - 90^\circ$ triangle, the three angles are 45°, $45^\circ$and 90°. The lengths of the sides of this triangle are in the ratio of $1:1:\sqrt{2}$.
- In a special triangle $30^\circ - 60^\circ - 90^\circ$, the three angles are $30^\circ - 60^\circ - 90^\circ$. The lengths of this triangle are in the ratio of $1:\sqrt{3}:2$.

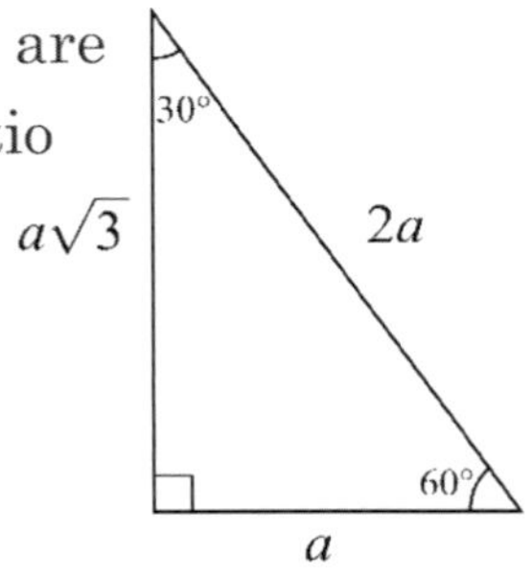

Examples:

Example 1. Find the length of the hypotenuse of a right triangle if the length of the other two sides are both 4 inches.

Solution: this is a right triangle with two equal sides. Therefore, it must be a $45^\circ - 45^\circ - 90^\circ$ triangle. Two equivalent sides are 4 inches. The ratio of sides: $x:x:x\sqrt{2}$

The length of the hypotenuse is $4\sqrt{2}$ inches. $x:x:x\sqrt{2} \rightarrow 4:4:4\sqrt{2}$

Example 2. The length of the hypotenuse of a right triangle is 6 inches. What are the lengths of the other two sides if one angle of the triangle is 30°?

Solution: The hypotenuse is 6 inches and the triangle is a $30^\circ - 60^\circ - 90^\circ$ triangle. Then, one side of the triangle is 3 (it's half the side of the hypotenuse) and the other side is $3\sqrt{3}$. (it's the smallest side times $\sqrt{3}$)

$x:x\sqrt{3}:2x \rightarrow x = 3 \rightarrow x:x\sqrt{3}:2x = 3:3\sqrt{3}:6$

Polygons

- The perimeter of a square $= 4 \times side = 4s$

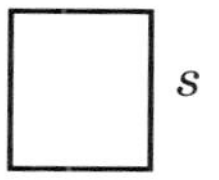

- The perimeter of a rectangle $= 2(width + length)$

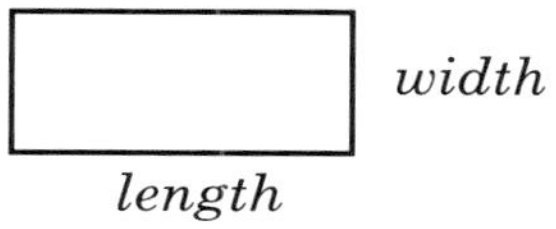

- The perimeter of trapezoid $= a + b + c + d$

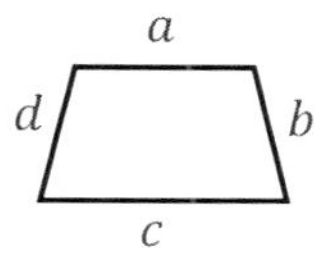

- The perimeter of a regular hexagon $= 6a$

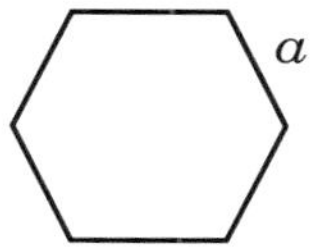

- The perimeter of a parallelogram $= 2(l + w)$

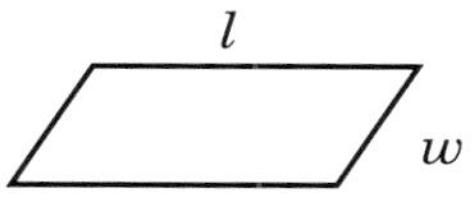

Examples:

Example 1. Find the perimeter of following regular hexagon.

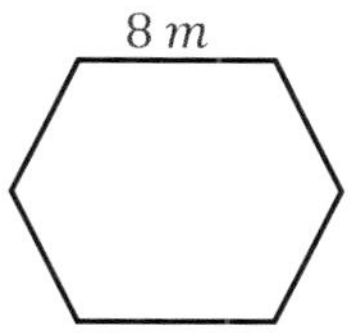

Solution: Since the hexagon is regular, all sides are equal.

Then, the perimeter of the hexagon $= 6 \times (one\ side)$

The perimeter of the hexagon $= 6 \times (one\ side) = 6 \times 8 = 48\ m$

Example 2. Find the perimeter of following trapezoid.

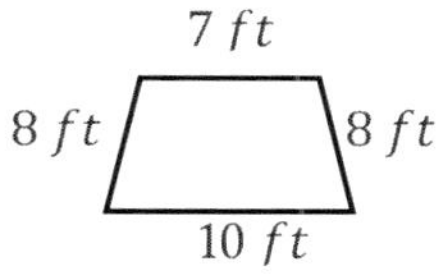

Solution: The perimeter of a trapezoid $= a + b + c + d$

The perimeter of the trapezoid $= 7 + 8 + 8 + 10 = 33\ ft$

Circles

- In a circle, variable r is usually used for the radius and d for diameter.
- $Area\ of\ a\ circle = \pi r^2$ (π is about 3.14)
- $Circumference\ of\ a\ circle = 2\pi r$

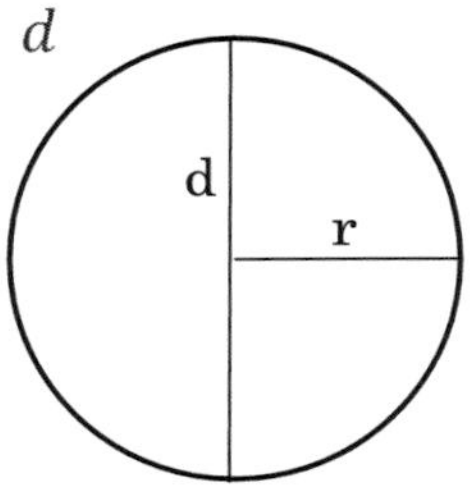

Examples:

Example 1. Find the area of this circle. ($\pi = 3.14$)

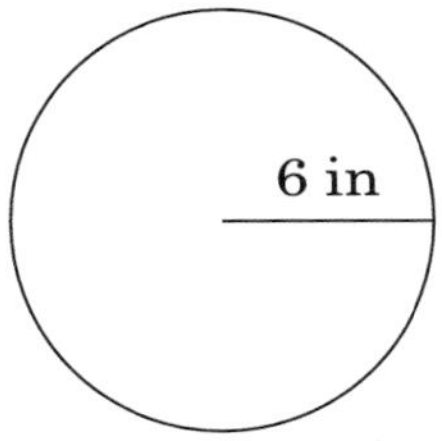

Solution:
Use area formula: $Area = \pi r^2$
$r = 6\ in \rightarrow Area = \pi(6)^2 = 36\pi,\ \pi = 3.14$
Then: $Area = 36 \times 3.14 = 113.04\ in^2$

Example 2. Find the Circumference of this circle. ($\pi = 3.14$)

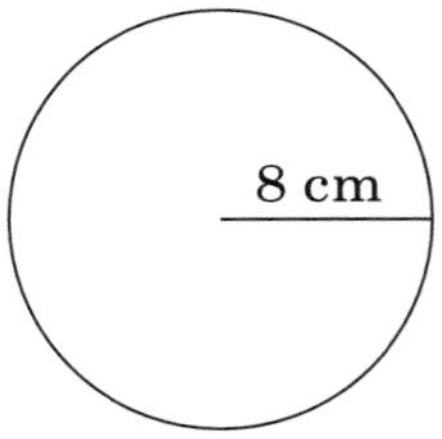

Solution:
Use Circumference formula: $Circumference = 2\pi r$
$r = 8\ cm \rightarrow Circumference = 2\pi(8) = 16\pi$
$\pi = 3.14$, Then: $Circumference = 16 \times 3.14 = 50.24\ cm$

Example 3. Find the area of this circle.

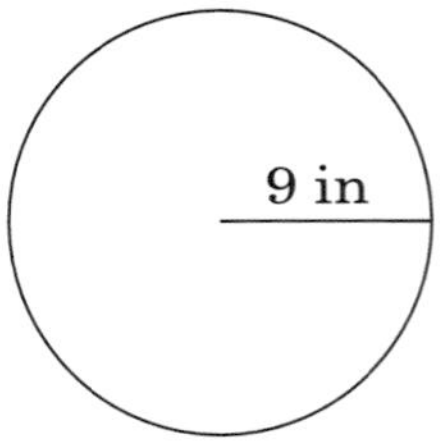

Solution:
Use area formula: $Area = \pi r^2$
$r = 9\ in$, Then: $Area = \pi(9)^2 = 81\pi,\ \pi = 3.14$
$Area = 81 \times 3.14 = 254.34\ in^2$

Trapezoids

- A quadrilateral with at least one pair of parallel sides is a trapezoid.

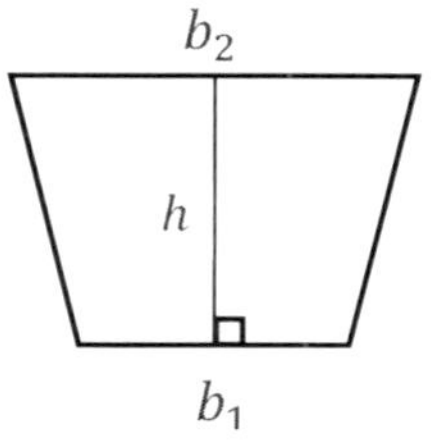

- Area of a trapezoid $= \frac{1}{2}h(b_1 + b_2)$

Examples:

Example 1. Calculate the area of this trapezoid.

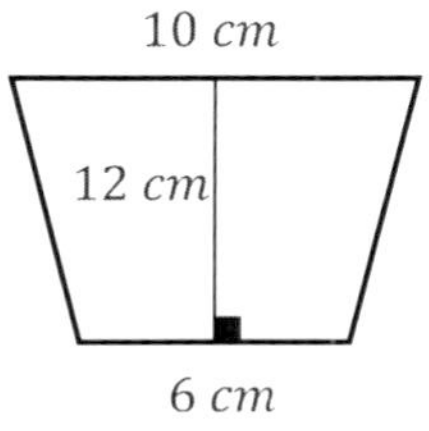

Solution:

Use area formula: $A = \frac{1}{2}h(b_1 + b_2)$

$b_1 = 6\ cm$, $b_2 = 10\ cm$ and $h = 12\ cm$

Then: $A = \frac{1}{2}(12)(10 + 6) = 6(16) = 96\ cm^2$

Example 2. Calculate the area of this trapezoid.

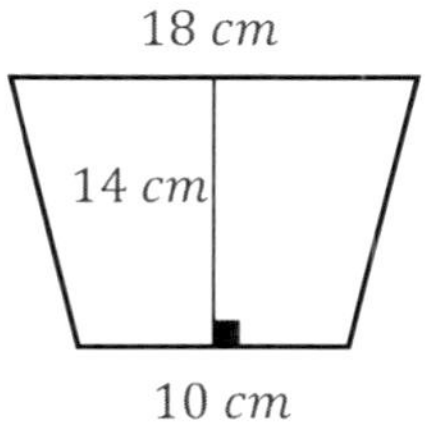

Solution:

Use area formula: $A = \frac{1}{2}h(b_1 + b_2)$

$b_1 = 10\ cm$, $b_2 = 18\ cm$ and $h = 14\ cm$

Then: $A = \frac{1}{2}(14)(10 + 18) = 196\ cm^2$

Cubes

- A cube is a three-dimensional solid object bounded by six square sides.
- Volume is the measure of the amount of space inside of a solid figure, like a cube, ball, cylinder or pyramid.
- The volume of a cube $= (one\ side)^3$
- The surface area of a cube $= 6 \times (one\ side)^2$

Examples:

Example 1. Find the volume and surface area of this cube.

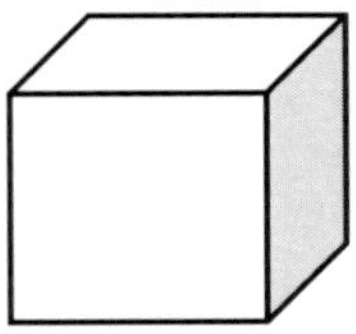

Solution: Use volume formula: $volume = (one\ side)^3$
Then: $volume = (one\ side)^3 = (3)^3 = 27\ cm^3$
Use surface area formula:
$surface\ area\ of\ a\ cube$: $6(one\ side)^2 = 6(3)^2 = 6(9) = 54\ cm^2$

Example 2. Find the volume and surface area of this cube.

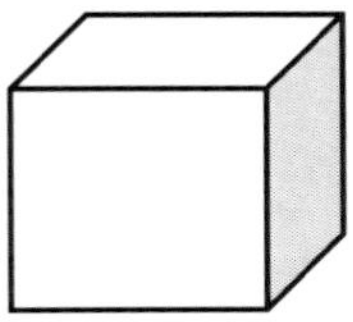

Solution: Use volume formula: $volume = (one\ side)^3$
Then: $volume = (one\ side)^3 = (6)^3 = 216\ cm^3$
Use surface area formula:
$surface\ area\ of\ a\ cube$: $6(one\ side)^2 = 6(6)^2 = 6(36) = 216\ cm^2$

Example 3. Find the volume and surface area of this cube.

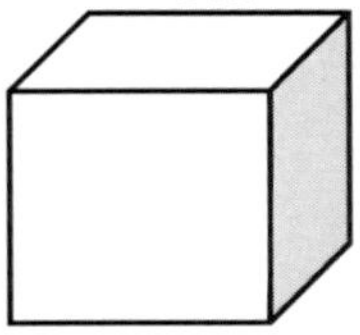

Solution: Use volume formula: $volume = (one\ side)^3$
Then: $volume = (one\ side)^3 = (8)^3 = 512\ m^3$
Use surface area formula:
$surface\ area\ of\ a\ cube$: $6(one\ side)^2 = 6(8)^2 = 6(64) = 384\ m^2$

Rectangular Prisms

- A rectangular prism is a solid 3-dimensional object with six rectangular faces.
- The volume of a Rectangular prism $= Length \times Width \times Height$

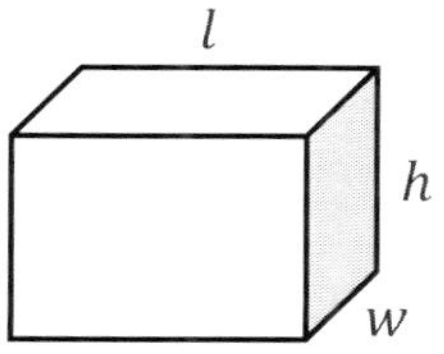

$Volume = l \times w \times h$

$Surface\ area = 2 \times (wh + lw + lh)$

Examples:

Example 1. Find the volume and surface area of this rectangular prism.

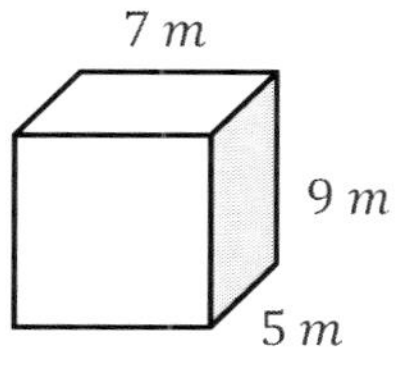

Solution: Use volume formula: $Volume = l \times w \times h$

Then: $Volume = 7 \times 5 \times 9 = 315\ m^3$

Use surface area formula: $Surface\ area = 2 \times (wh + lw + lh)$

Then: $Surface\ area = 2 \times \big((5 \times 9) + (7 \times 5) + (7 \times 9)\big)$

$= 2 \times (45 + 35 + 63) = 2 \times (143) = 286\ m^2$

Example 2. Find the volume and surface area of this rectangular prism.

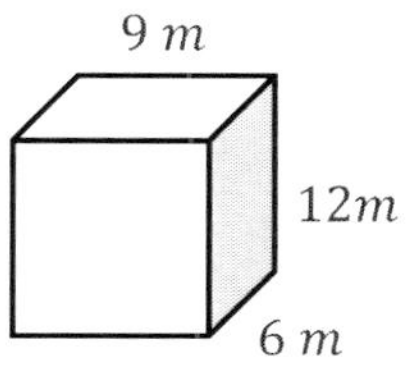

Solution: Use volume formula: $Volume = l \times w \times h$

Then: $Volume = 9 \times 6 \times 12 = 648\ m^3$

Use surface area formula: $Surface\ area = 2 \times (wh + lw + lh)$

Then: $Surface\ area = 2 \times \big((6 \times 12) + (9 \times 6) + (9 \times 12)\big)$

$= 2 \times (72 + 54 + 108) = 2 \times (234) = 468\ m^2$

Cylinder

- A cylinder is a solid geometric figure with straight parallel sides and a circular or oval cross-section.
- $Volume\ of\ a\ Cylinder = \pi(radius)^2 \times height,\ \pi \approx 3.14$
- $Surface\ area\ of\ a\ cylinder = 2\pi r^2 + 2\pi rh$

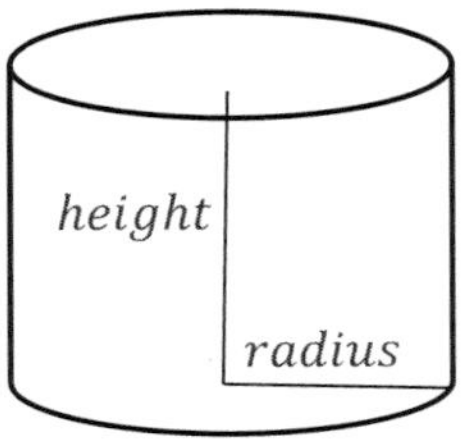

Examples:

Example 1. Find the volume and Surface area of the follow Cylinder.

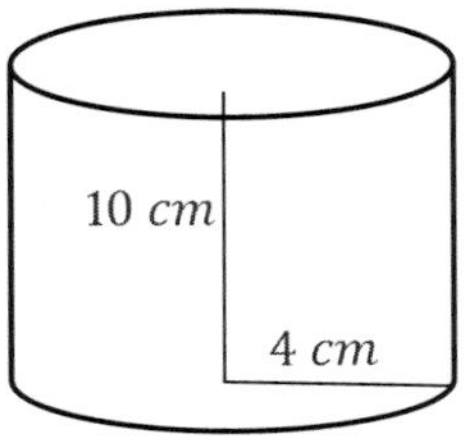

Solution: Use volume formula:

$Volume = \pi(radius)^2 \times height$

Then: $Volume = \pi(4)^2 \times 10 = 16\pi \times 10 = 160\pi$

$\pi = 3.14$, then: $Volume = 160\pi = 160 \times 3.14 = 502.4\ cm^3$

Use surface area formula: $Surface\ area = 2\pi r^2 + 2\pi rh$

Then: $2\pi(4)^2 + 2\pi(4)(10) = 2\pi(16) + 2\pi(40) = 32\pi + 80\pi = 112\pi$

$\pi = 3.14$, Then: $Surface\ area = 112 \times 3.14 = 351.68\ cm^2$

Example 2. Find the volume and Surface area of the follow Cylinder.

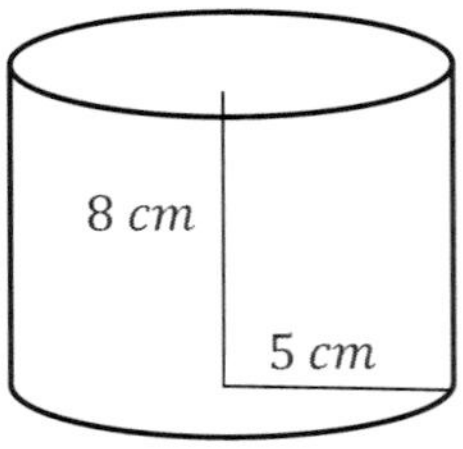

Solution: Use volume formula:

$Volume = \pi(radius)^2 \times height$

Then: $Volume = \pi(5)^2 \times 8 = 25\,\pi \times 8 = 200\pi$

$\pi = 3.14$, Then: $Volume = 200\pi = 628\ cm^3$

Use surface area formula: $Surface\ area = 2\pi r^2 + 2\pi rh$

Then: $= 2\pi(5)^2 + 2\pi(5)(8) = 2\pi(25) + 2\pi(40) = 50\pi + 80\pi = 130\pi$

$\pi = 3.14$ then: $Surface\ area = 130 \times 3.14 = 408.2\ cm^2$

Chapter 11: Practices

Find the missing side?

1)

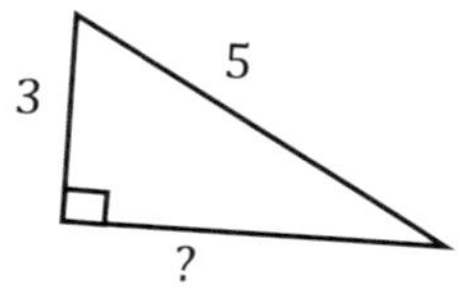

2)

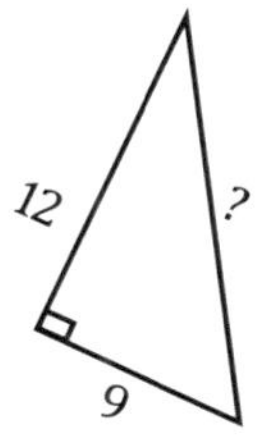

3)

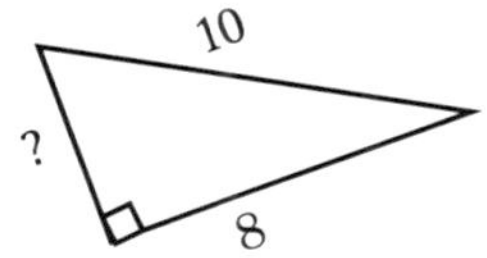

4)

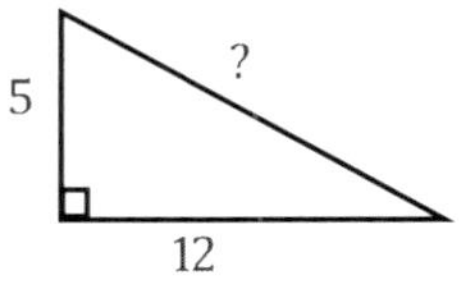

Find the measure of the unknown angle in each triangle.

5)

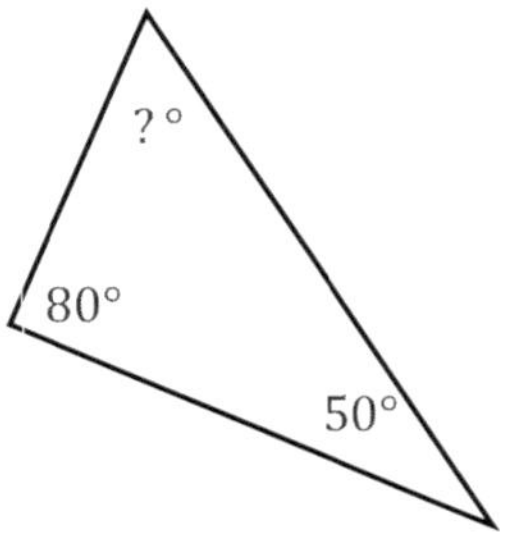

6)

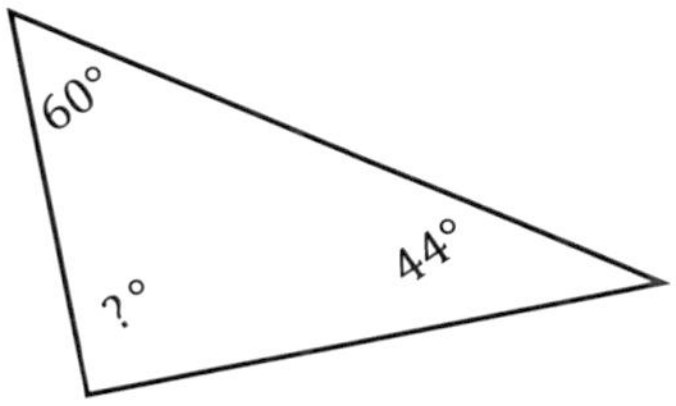

7)

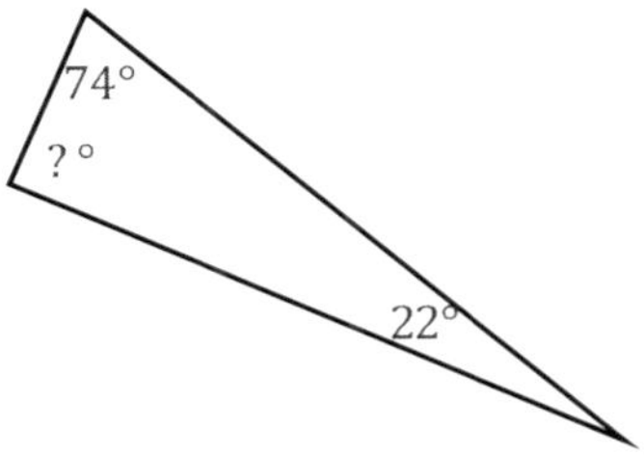

8)

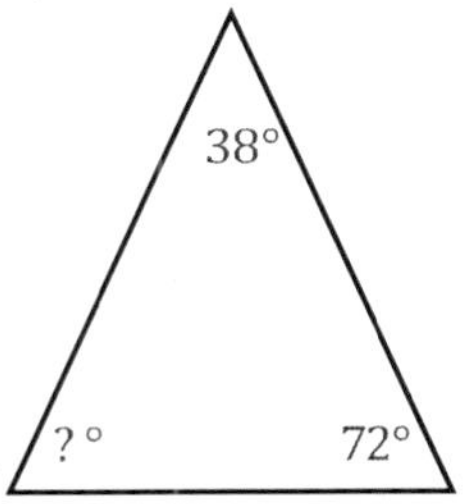

Find the area of each triangle.

9)

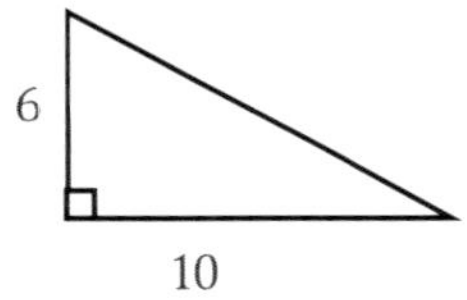

10)

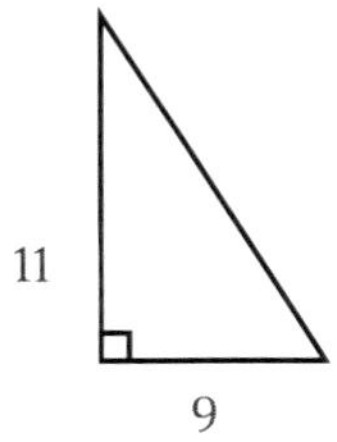

11)

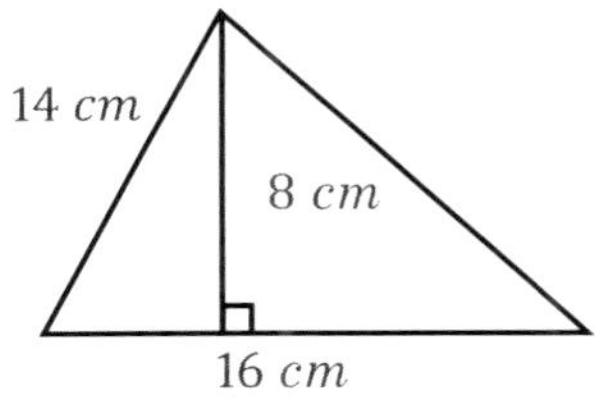

12)

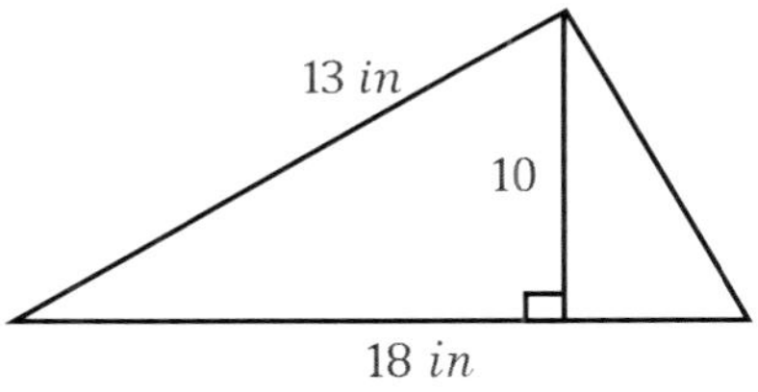

Find the perimeter or circumference of each shape.

13)

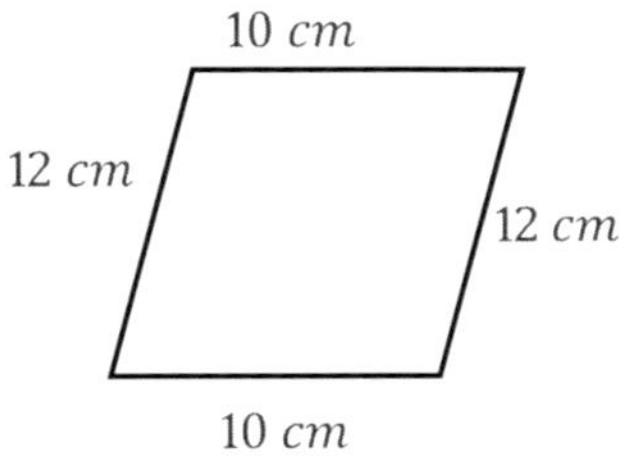

14)

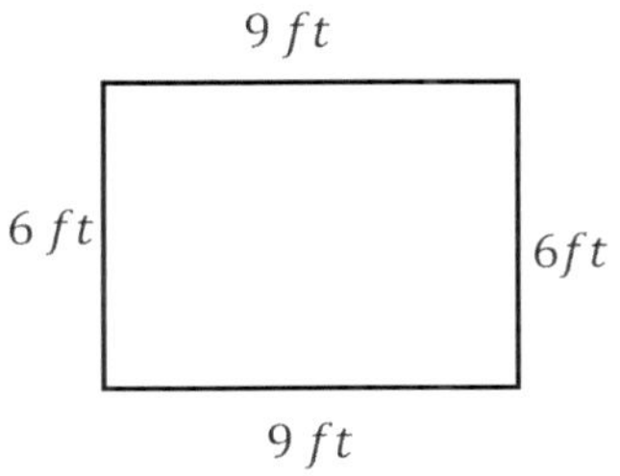

15)

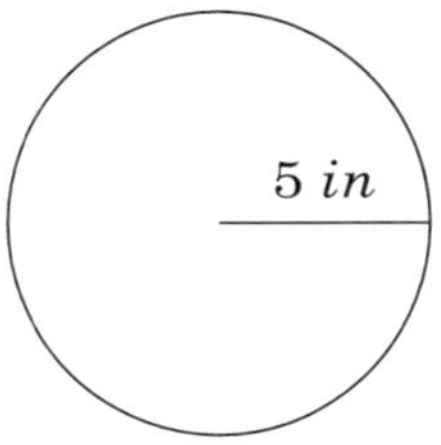

16) *regular hexagon*

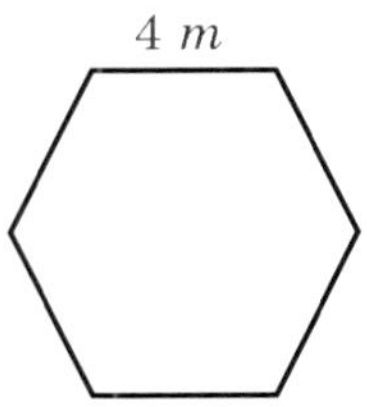

Find the area of each trapezoid.

17)

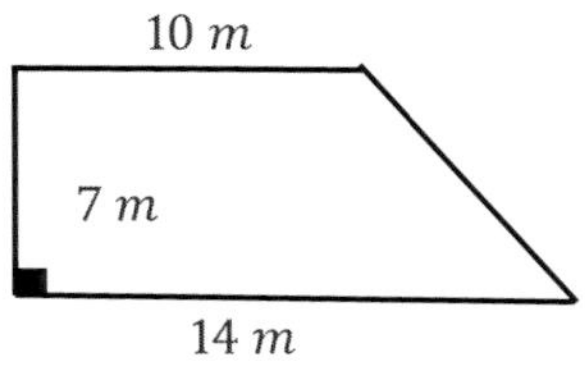

18)

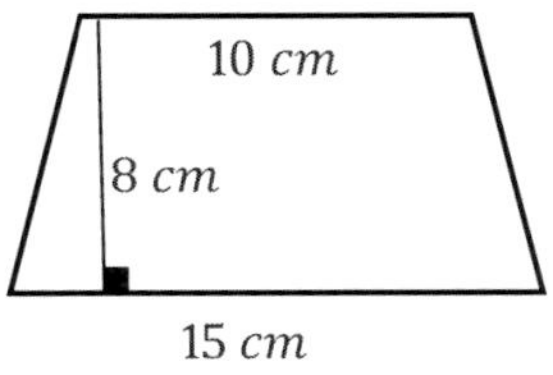

19)

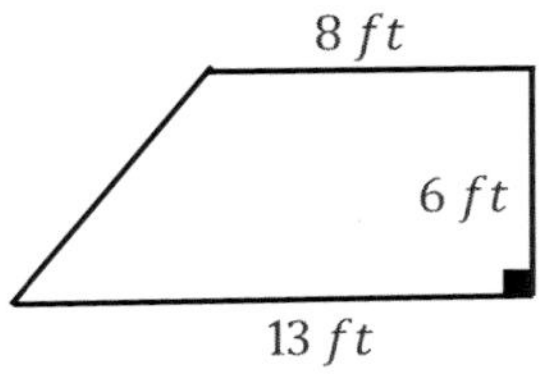

20)

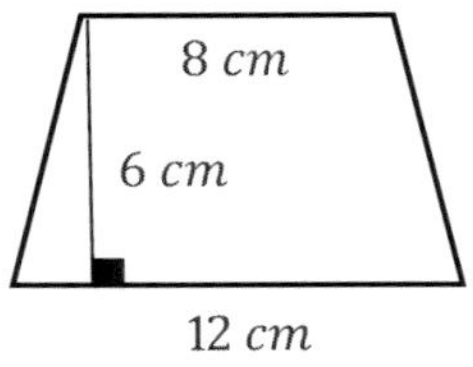

Find the volume of each cube.

21)

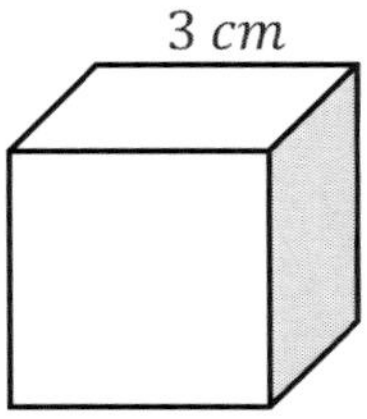

22)

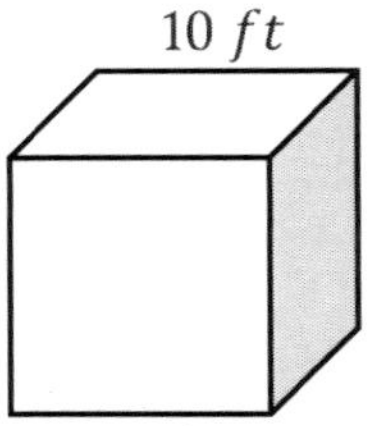

23)

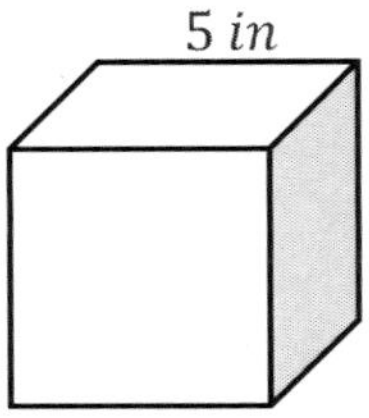

24)

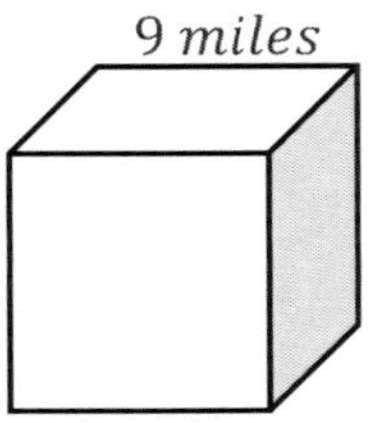

Find the volume of each Rectangular Prism.

25)

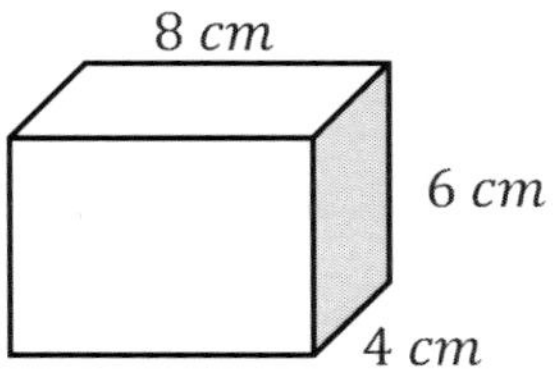

26)

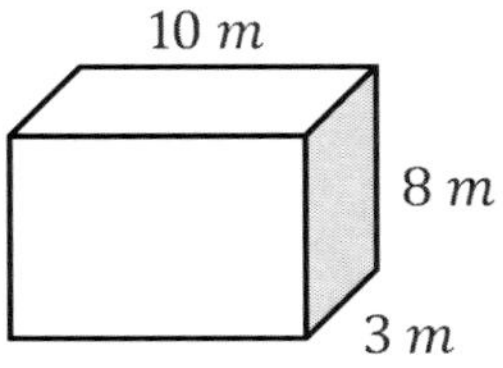

27)

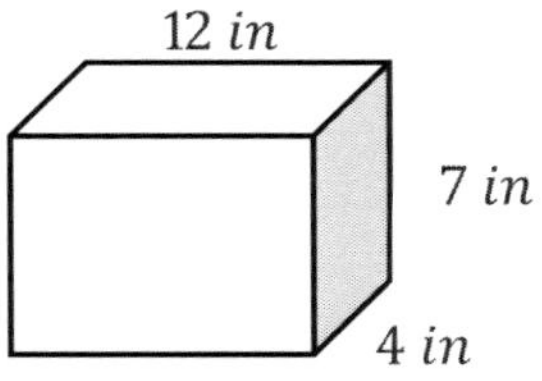

Find the volume of each Cylinder. Round your answer to the nearest tenth. ($\pi = 3.14$)

28)

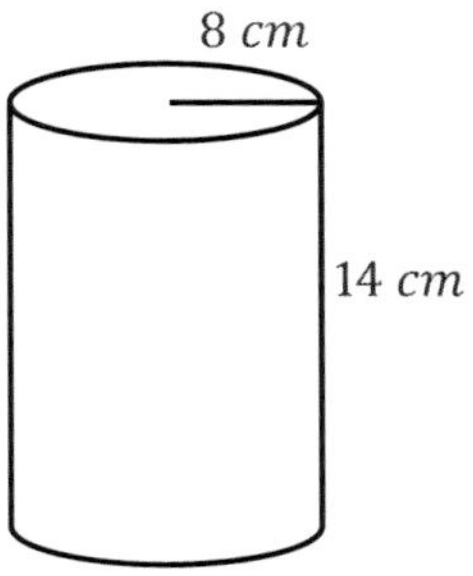

29)

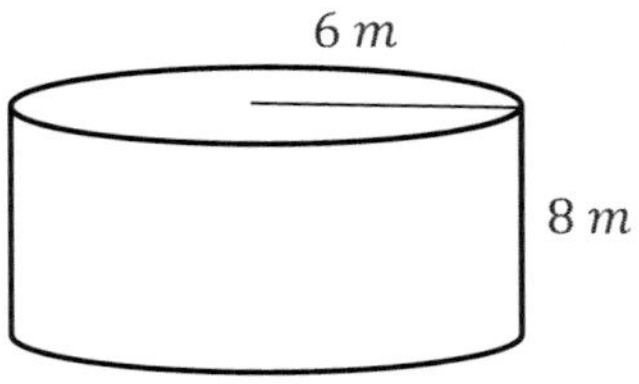

30)

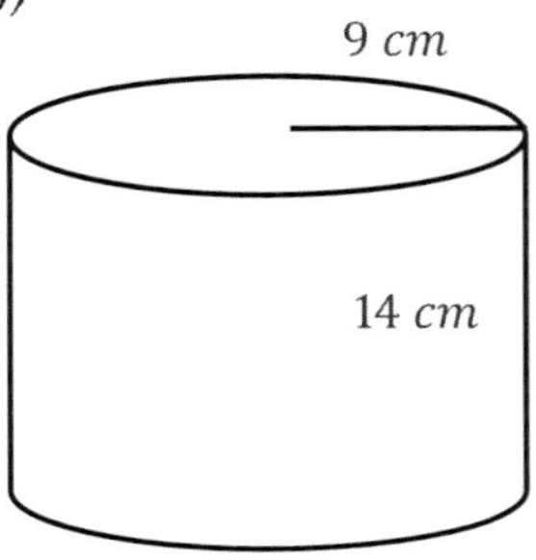

Chapter 11: Answers

1) 4	11) 64 cm^2	21) 27 cm^3
2) 15	12) 90 in^2	22) 1,000 ft^3
3) 6	13) 44 cm	23) 125 in^3
4) 13	14) 30 ft	24) 729 mi^3
5) 50	15) 10 $\pi \approx 31.4\ in$	25) 192 cm^3
6) 76	16) 24 m	26) 240 m^3
7) 84	17) 84 m^2	27) 336 in^3
8) 70	18) 100 cm^2	28) 2,813.44 cm^3
9) 30	19) 63 ft^2	29) 904.32 m^3
10) 49.5	20) 60 cm^2	30) 3,560.76 cm^3

CHAPTER

12 Statistics

Math topics that you'll learn in this chapter:

- ☑ Mean, Median, Mode, and Range of the Given Data
- ☑ Pie Graph
- ☑ Probability Problems
- ☑ Permutations and Combinations

Mean, Median, Mode, and Range of the Given Data

- **Mean:** $\frac{\textit{sum of the data}}{\textit{total number of data entires}}$
- **Mode:** the value in the list that appears most often
- **Median:** is the middle number of a group of numbers arranged in order by size.
- **Range:** the difference of the largest value and smallest value in the list

Examples:

Example 1. What is the mode of these numbers? $5, 6, 8, 6, 8, 5, 3, 5$

Solution: Mode: the value in the list that appears most often.
Therefore, the mode is number 5. There are three number 5 in the data.

Example 2. What is the median of these numbers? $6, 11, 15, 10, 17, 20, 7$

Solution: Write the numbers in order: $6, 7, 10, 11, 15, 17, 20$
The median is the number in the middle. Therefore, the median is 11.

Example 3. What is the mean of these numbers? $7, 2, 3, 2, 4, 8, 7, 5$

Solution: Mean: $\frac{\textit{sum of the data}}{\textit{total number of data entires}} = \frac{7+2+3+2+4+8+7+5}{8} = \frac{38}{8} = 4.75$

Example 4. What is the range in this list? $3, 7, 12, 6, 15, 20, 8$

Solution: Range is the difference of the largest value and smallest value in the list. The largest value is 20 and the smallest value is 3.
Then: $20 - 3 = 17$

Find more at bit.ly/2KO86gg

Pie Graph

- A Pie Graph (Pie Chart) is a circle chart divided into sectors, each sector represents the relative size of each value.
- Pie charts represent a snapshot of how a group is broken down into smaller pieces.

Examples:

A library has 750 books that include Mathematics, Physics, Chemistry, English and History. Use the following graph to answer the questions.

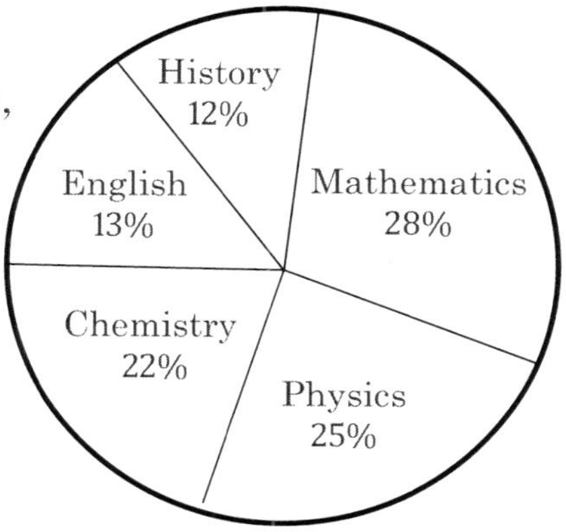

Example 1. What is the number of Mathematics books?

Solution: Number of total books $= 750$

Percent of Mathematics books $= 28\%$

Then, the number of Mathematics books: $28\% \times 750 = 0.28 \times 750 = 210$

Example 2. What is the number of History books?

Solution: Number of total books $= 750$

Percent of History books $= 12\%$

Then: $0.12 \times 750 = 90$

Example 3. What is the number of Chemistry books in the library?

Solution: Number of total books $= 750$

Percent of Chemistry books $= 22\%$

Then: $0.22 \times 750 = 165$

Probability Problems

- Probability is the likelihood of something happening in the future. It is expressed as a number between zero (can never happen) to 1 (will always happen).
- Probability can be expressed as a fraction, a decimal, or a percent.
- Probability formula: $Probability = \frac{number\ of\ desired\ outcomes}{number\ of\ total\ outcomes}$

Examples:

Example 1. Anita's trick–or–treat bag contains 10 pieces of chocolate, 16 suckers, 16 pieces of gum, 22 pieces of licorice. If she randomly pulls a piece of candy from her bag, what is the probability of her pulling out a piece of sucker?

Solution: Probability $= \frac{number\ of\ desired\ outcomes}{\text{number of total outcomes}}$

Probability of pulling out a piece of sucker $= \frac{16}{10 + 16 + 16 + 22} = \frac{16}{64} = \frac{1}{4}$

Example 2. A bag contains 20 balls: four green, five black, eight blue, a brown, a red and one white. If 19 balls are removed from the bag at random, what is the probability that a brown ball has been removed?

Solution: If 19 balls are removed from the bag at random, there will be one ball in the bag. The probability of choosing a brown ball is 1 out of 20. Therefore, the probability of not choosing a brown ball is 19 out of 20 and the probability of having not a brown ball after removing 19 balls is the same. The answer is: $\frac{19}{20}$

Permutations and Combinations

Factorials are products, indicated by an exclamation mark. For example, $4! = 4 \times 3 \times 2 \times 1$ (Remember that 0! is defined to be equal to 1)

- **Permutations:** The number of ways to choose a sample of k elements from a set of n distinct objects where order does matter, and replacements are not allowed. For a permutation problem, use this formula:

$$_{n}P_{k} = \frac{n!}{(n-k)!}$$

- **Combination:** The number of ways to choose a sample of r elements from a set of n distinct objects where order does not matter, and replacements are not allowed. For a combination problem, use this formula:

$$_{n}C_{r} = \frac{n!}{r!\,(n-r)!}$$

Examples:

Example 1. How many ways can the first and second place be awarded to 7 people?

Solution: Since the order matters, (the first and second place are different!) we need to use permutation formula where n is 7 and k is 2. Then: $\frac{n!}{(n-k)!} = \frac{7!}{(7-2)!} = \frac{7!}{5!} = \frac{7\times6\times5!}{5!}$, remove 5! from both sides of the fraction. Then: $\frac{7\times6\times5!}{5!} = 7 \times 6 = 42$

Example 2. How many ways can we pick a team of 3 people from a group of 8?

Solution: Since the order doesn't matter, we need to use a combination formula where n is 8 and r is 3.

Then: $\frac{n!}{r!\,(n-r)!} = \frac{8!}{3!\,(8-3)!} = \frac{8!}{3!\,(5)!} = \frac{8\times7\times6\times5!}{3!\,(5)!} = \frac{8\times7\times6}{3\times2\times1} = \frac{336}{6} = 56$

Chapter 12: Practices

Find the values of the Given Data.

1) 6, 11, 5, 3, 6

Mode: _____ Range: _____

Mean: _____ Median: _____

2) 4, 9, 1, 9, 6, 7

Mode: _____ Range: _____

Mean: _____ Median: _____

3) 10, 3, 6, 10, 4, 15

Mode: _____ Range: _____

Mean: _____ Median: _____

4) 12, 4, 8, 9, 3, 12, 15

Mode: _____ Range: _____

Mean: _____ Median: _____

The circle graph below shows all Bob's expenses for last month. Bob spent $790 on his Rent last month.

5) How much did Bob's total expenses last month? ________

6) How much did Bob spend for foods last month? ________

7) How much did Bob spend for his bills last month? ________

8) How much did Bob spend on his car last month? ________

Bob's last month expenses

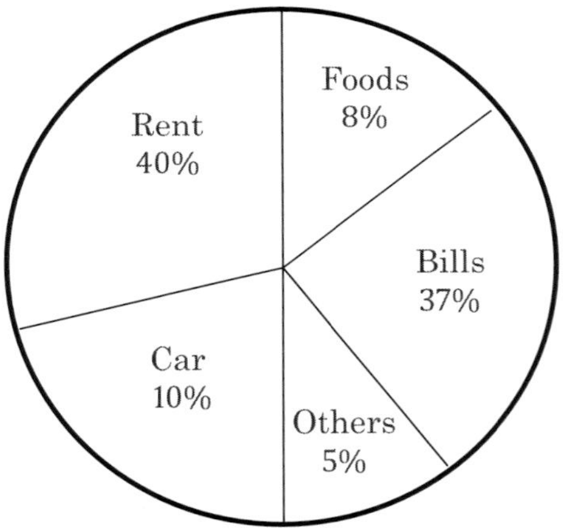

Solve.

9) Bag A contains 8 red marbles and 6 green marbles. Bag B contains 5 black marbles and 7 orange marbles. What is the probability of selecting a green marble at random from bag A? What is the probability of selecting a black marble at random from Bag B?

______________ ______________

Solve.

10) Susan is baking cookies. She uses sugar, flour, butter, and eggs. How many different orders of ingredients can she try? ______________

11) Jason is planning for his vacation. He wants to go to museum, go to the beach, and play volleyball. How many different ways of ordering are there for him? ______________

12) In how many ways can a team of 6 basketball players choose a captain and co-captain? ______________

13) How many ways can you give 5 balls to your 8 friends? ______________

14) A professor is going to arrange her 5 students in a straight line. In how many ways can she do this? ______________

15) In how many ways can a teacher chooses 12 out of 15 students? ______________

Chapter 12: Answers

1) Mode: 6, Range: 8, Mean: 6.2, Median: 6

2) Mode: 9, Range:8, Mean: 6, Median: 6.5

3) Mode: 10, Range: 12, Mean: 8, Median: 8

4) Mode: 12, Range: 12, Mean: 9, Median: 9

5) $1,975

6) $158

7) $730.75

8) $197.50

9) $\frac{3}{7}, \frac{5}{12}$

10) 24

11) 6

12) 30 (it's a permutation problem)

13) 56 (it's a combination problem)

14) 120

15) 455 (it's a combination problem)

CHAPTER

13 Functions Operations

Math topics that you'll learn in this chapter:

- ☑ Function Notation and Evaluation
- ☑ Adding and Subtracting Functions
- ☑ Multiplying and Dividing Functions
- ☑ Composition of Functions

Function Notation and Evaluation

- Functions are mathematical operations that assign unique outputs to given inputs.
- Function notation is the way a function is written. It is meant to be a precise way of giving information about the function without a rather lengthy written explanation.
- The most popular function notation is $f(x)$ which is read "f of x". Any letter can name a function. for example: $g(x)$, $h(x)$, etc.
- To evaluate a function, plug in the input (the given value or expression) for the function's variable (place holder, x).

Examples:

Example 1. Evaluate: $f(x) = x + 6$, find $f(2)$

Solution: Substitute x with 2:
Then: $f(x) = x + 6 \rightarrow f(2) = 2 + 6 \rightarrow f(2) = 8$

Example 2. Evaluate: $w(x) = 3x - 1$, find $w(4)$.

Solution: Substitute x with 4:
Then: $w(x) = 3x - 1 \rightarrow w(4) = 3(4) - 1 = 12 - 1 = 11$

Example 3. Evaluate: $f(x) = 2x^2 + 4$, find $f(-1)$.

Solution: Substitute x with -1:
Then: $f(x) = 2x^2 + 4 \rightarrow f(-1) = 2(-1)^2 + 4 \rightarrow f(-1) = 2 + 4 = 6$

Example 4. Evaluate: $h(x) = 4x^2 - 9$, find $h(2a)$.

Solution: Substitute x with $2a$:
Then: $h(x) = 4x^2 - 9 \rightarrow h(2a) = 4(2a)^2 - 9 \rightarrow h(2a) = 4(4a^2) - 9 = 16a^2 - 9$

Adding and Subtracting Functions

- Just like we can add and subtract numbers and expressions, we can add or subtract functions and simplify or evaluate them. The result is a new function.
- For two functions $f(x)$ and $g(x)$, we can create two new functions:

$$(f+g)(x) = f(x) + g(x) \text{ and } (f-g)(x) = f(x) - g(x)$$

Examples:

Example 1. $g(x) = 2x - 2$, $f(x) = x + 1$, Find: $(g+f)(x)$

Solution: $(g+f)(x) = g(x) + f(x)$
Then: $(g+f)(x) = (2x-2) + (x+1) = 2x - 2 + x + 1 = 3x - 1$

Example 2. $f(x) = 4x - 3$, $g(x) = 2x - 4$, Find: $(f-g)(x)$

Solution: $(f-g)(x) = f(x) - g(x)$
Then: $(f-g)(x) = (4x-3) - (2x-4) = 4x - 3 - 2x + 4 = 2x + 1$

Example 3. $g(x) = x^2 + 2$, $f(x) = x + 5$, Find: $(g+f)(x)$

Solution: $(g+f)(x) = g(x) + f(x)$
Then: $(g+f)(x) = (x^2+2) + (x+5) = x^2 + x + 7$

Example 4. $f(x) = 5x^2 - 3$, $g(x) = 3x + 6$, Find: $(f-g)(3)$

Solution: $(f-g)(x) = f(x) - g(x)$
Then: $(f-g)(x) = (5x^2-3) - (3x+6) = 5x^2 - 3 - 3x - 6 = 5x^2 - 3x - 9$
Substitute x with 3: $(f-g)(3) = 5(3)^2 - 3(3) - 9 = 45 - 9 - 9 = 27$

bit.ly/3hdeFVO
Find more at

Multiplying and Dividing Functions

- Just like we can multiply and divide numbers and expressions, we can multiply and divide two functions and simplify or evaluate them.
- For two functions $f(x)$ and $g(x)$, we can create two new functions:

$$(f.g)(x) = f(x).g(x) \text{ and } \left(\frac{f}{g}\right)(x) = \frac{f(x)}{g(x)}$$

Examples:

Example 1. $g(x) = x + 3$, $f(x) = x + 4$, Find: $(g.f)(x)$

Solution:

$$(g.f)(x) = g(x).f(x) = (x+3)(x+4) = x^2 + 4x + 3x + 12 = x^2 + 7x + 12$$

Example 2. $f(x) = x + 6$, $h(x) = x - 9$, Find: $\left(\frac{f}{h}\right)(x)$

Solution: $\left(\frac{f}{h}\right)(x) = \frac{f(x)}{h(x)} = \frac{x+6}{x-9}$

Example 3. $g(x) = x + 7$, $f(x) = x - 3$, Find: $(g.f)(2)$

Solution: $(g.f)(x) = g(x).f(x) = (x+7)(x-3) = x^2 - 3x + 7x - 21$

$$g(x).f(x) = x^2 + 4x - 21$$

Substitute x with 2: $(g.f)(x) = (2)^2 + 4(2) - 21 = 4 + 8 - 21 = -9$

Example 4. $f(x) = x + 3$, $h(x) = 2x - 4$, Find: $\left(\frac{f}{h}\right)(3)$

Solution: $\left(\frac{f}{h}\right)(x) = \frac{f(x)}{h(x)} = \frac{x+3}{2x-4}$

Substitute x with 3: $\left(\frac{f}{h}\right)(x) = \frac{x+3}{2x-4} = \frac{3+3}{2(3)-4} = \frac{6}{2} = 3$

Composition of Functions

- "Composition of functions" simply means combining two or more functions in a way where the output from one function becomes the input for the next function.
- The notation used for composition is: $(fog)(x) = f(g(x))$ and is read "f composed with g of x" or "f of g of x".

Examples:

Example 1. Using $f(x) = 2x + 3$ and $g(x) = 5x$, find: $(fog)(x)$

Solution: $(fog)(x) = f(g(x))$. Then: $(fog)(x) = f(g(x)) = f(5x)$

Now find $f(5x)$ by substituting x with $5x$ in $f(x)$ function.

Then: $f(x) = 2x + 3$; $(x \rightarrow 5x) \rightarrow f(5x) = 2(5x) + 3 = 10x + 3$

Example 2. Using $f(x) = 3x - 1$ and $g(x) = 2x - 2$, find: $(gof)(5)$

Solution: $(fog)(x) = f(g(x))$. Then: $(gof)(x) = g(f(x)) = g(3x - 1)$,

Now substitute x in $g(x)$ *by* $(3x - 1)$.

Then: $g(3x - 1) = 2(3x - 1) - 2 = 6x - 2 - 2 = 6x - 4$

Substitute x with 5: $(gof)(5) = g(f(x)) = 6x - 4 = 6(5) - 4 = 26$

Example 3. Using $f(x) = 2x^2 - 5$ and $g(x) = x + 3$, find: $f(g(3))$

Solution: First, find $g(3)$: $g(x) = x + 3 \rightarrow g(3) = 3 + 3 = 6$

Then: $f(g(3)) = f(6)$. Now, find $f(6)$ by substituting x with 6 in $f(x)$ function.

$f(g(3)) = f(6) = 2(6)^2 - 5 = 2(36) - 5 = 67$

Chapter 13: Practices

Evaluate each function.

1) $g(n) = 2n + 5$, find $g(2)$

_____

2) $h(x) = 5x - 9$, find $h(4)$

_____

3) $k(n) = 10 - 6n$, find $k(2)$

_____

4) $g(x) = -5x + 6$, find $g(-2)$

_____

5) $k(n) = -8n + 3$, find $k(-6)$

_____

6) $w(n) = -2n - 9$, find $w(-5)$

_____

Perform the indicated operation.

7) $f(x) = x + 6$
$g(x) = 3x + 2$
Find $(f - g)(x)$

_____

8) $g(x) = x - 9$
$f(x) = 2x - 1$
Find $(g - f)(x)$

_____

9) $h(t) = 5t + 6$
$g(t) = 2t + 4$
Find $(h + g)(x)$

_____

10) $g(a) = -6a + 1$
$f(a) = 3a^2 - 3$
Find $(g + f)(5)$

_____

11) $g(x) = 7x - 1$
$h(x) = -4x^2 + 2$
Find $(g - h)(-3)$

_____

12) $h(x) = -x^2 - 1$
$g(x) = -7x - 1$
Find $(h - g)(-5)$

_____

Perform the indicated operation.

13) $g(x) = x + 3$

$f(x) = x + 1$

Find $(g.f)(x)$

_____

14) $f(x) = 4x$

$h(x) = x - 6$

Find $(f.h)(x)$

_____

15) $g(a) = a - 8$

$h(a) = 4a - 2$

Find $(g.h)(3)$

_____

16) $f(x) = 6x + 2$

$h(x) = 5x - 1$

Find $\left(\frac{f}{h}\right)(-2)$

_____

17) $f(x) = 7a - 1$

$g(x) = -5 - 2a$

Find $\left(\frac{f}{g}\right)(-4)$

_____

18) $g(a) = a^2 - 4$

$f(a) = a + 6$

Find $\left(\frac{g}{f}\right)(-3)$

_____

Using $f(x) = 4x + 3$ and $g(x) = x - 7$, find:

19) $g(f(2)) =$_____

20) $g(f(-2)) =$_____

21) $f(g(4)) =$_____

22) $f(f(7)) =$_____

23) $g(f(5)) =$_____

24) $g(f(-5)) =$_____

25) $g(f(7)) =$ ____

26) $g(f(-3)) =$ ____

27) $f(g(-6)) =$ ____

Chapter 13: Answers

1) 9
2) 11
3) -2
4) 16
5) 51
6) 1
7) $-2x + 4$
8) $-x - 8$
9) $7t + 10$
10) 43
11) 12
12) -60
13) $x^2 + 4x + 3$
14) $4x^2 - 24x$
15) -50
16) $\frac{10}{11}$
17) $-\frac{29}{3}$
18) $\frac{5}{3}$
19) 4
20) -12
21) -9
22) 127
23) 16
24) -24
25) 24
26) -16
27) -49

Time to Test

Time to refine your Mathematics skill with a practice test

In this section, there are two complete SHSAT Mathematics practice tests. Take these tests to simulate the test day experience. After you've finished, score your tests using the answer keys.

Before You Start

- You'll need a pencil and a timer to take the test.
- It's okay to guess. There is no penalty for wrong answers.
- Use the answer sheet provided to record your answers.
- After you've finished the test, review the answer key to see where you went wrong.
- For each multiple-choice question, there are four possible answers. Choose which one is best. For grids in questions, write your answer in the answer boxes at the top of the grid. Then, as shown below fill in a bubble under each box in which you wrote your answer.

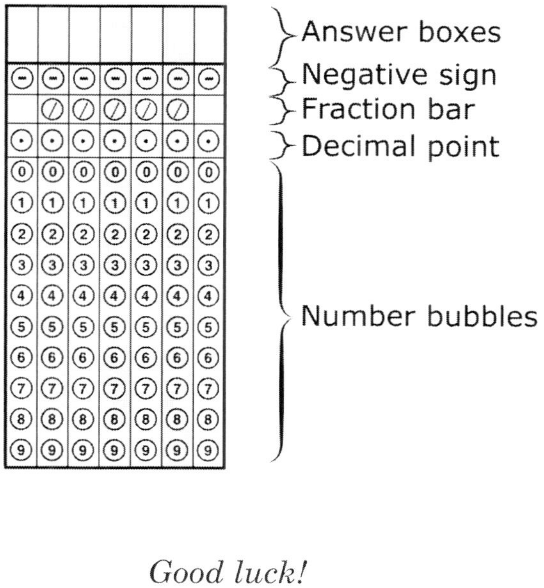

Good luck!

SHSAT Mathematics
Practice Test 1

2022

Total number of questions: 57

Total time for two parts: 75 Minutes

You may NOT use a calculator on this Test.

SHSAT Practice Tests Answer Sheet

Remove (or photocopy) these answer sheets and use them to complete the practice tests.

SHSAT Practice Test 1: Grid-ins Questions Answer Sheet

1

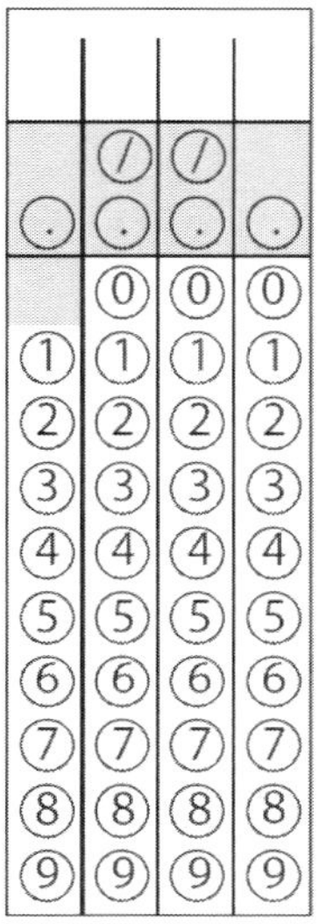

2

3

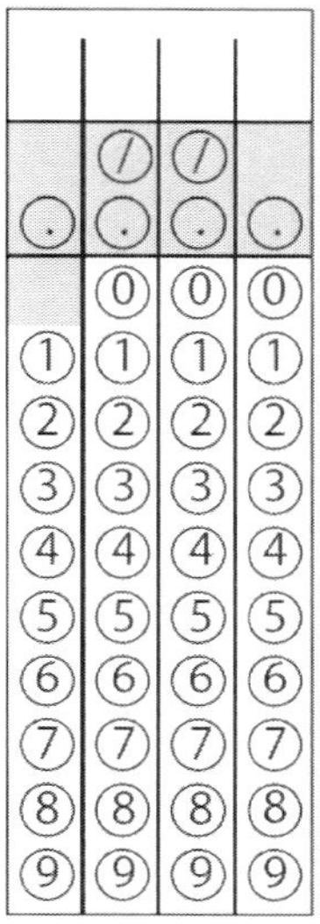

4

5

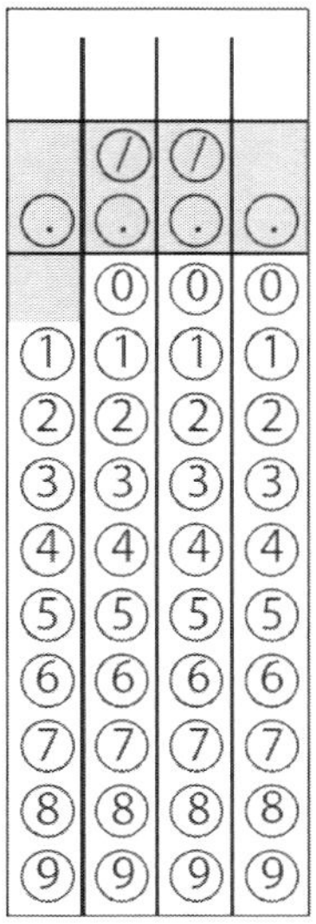

SHSAT Practice Test 1 – Multiple Choice Questions Answer Sheet

6	Ⓐ Ⓑ Ⓒ Ⓓ	18	Ⓐ Ⓑ Ⓒ Ⓓ	30	Ⓐ Ⓑ Ⓒ Ⓓ	42	Ⓐ Ⓑ Ⓒ Ⓓ	54	Ⓐ Ⓑ Ⓒ Ⓓ
7	Ⓐ Ⓑ Ⓒ Ⓓ	19	Ⓐ Ⓑ Ⓒ Ⓓ	31	Ⓐ Ⓑ Ⓒ Ⓓ	43	Ⓐ Ⓑ Ⓒ Ⓓ	55	Ⓐ Ⓑ Ⓒ Ⓓ
8	Ⓐ Ⓑ Ⓒ Ⓓ	20	Ⓐ Ⓑ Ⓒ Ⓓ	32	Ⓐ Ⓑ Ⓒ Ⓓ	44	Ⓐ Ⓑ Ⓒ Ⓓ	56	Ⓐ Ⓑ Ⓒ Ⓓ
9	Ⓐ Ⓑ Ⓒ Ⓓ	21	Ⓐ Ⓑ Ⓒ Ⓓ	33	Ⓐ Ⓑ Ⓒ Ⓓ	45	Ⓐ Ⓑ Ⓒ Ⓓ	57	Ⓐ Ⓑ Ⓒ Ⓓ
10	Ⓐ Ⓑ Ⓒ Ⓓ	22	Ⓐ Ⓑ Ⓒ Ⓓ	34	Ⓐ Ⓑ Ⓒ Ⓓ	46	Ⓐ Ⓑ Ⓒ Ⓓ		
11	Ⓐ Ⓑ Ⓒ Ⓓ	23	Ⓐ Ⓑ Ⓒ Ⓓ	35	Ⓐ Ⓑ Ⓒ Ⓓ	47	Ⓐ Ⓑ Ⓒ Ⓓ		
12	Ⓐ Ⓑ Ⓒ Ⓓ	24	Ⓐ Ⓑ Ⓒ Ⓓ	36	Ⓐ Ⓑ Ⓒ Ⓓ	48	Ⓐ Ⓑ Ⓒ Ⓓ		
13	Ⓐ Ⓑ Ⓒ Ⓓ	25	Ⓐ Ⓑ Ⓒ Ⓓ	37	Ⓐ Ⓑ Ⓒ Ⓓ	49	Ⓐ Ⓑ Ⓒ Ⓓ		
14	Ⓐ Ⓑ Ⓒ Ⓓ	26	Ⓐ Ⓑ Ⓒ Ⓓ	38	Ⓐ Ⓑ Ⓒ Ⓓ	50	Ⓐ Ⓑ Ⓒ Ⓓ		
15	Ⓐ Ⓑ Ⓒ Ⓓ	27	Ⓐ Ⓑ Ⓒ Ⓓ	39	Ⓐ Ⓑ Ⓒ Ⓓ	51	Ⓐ Ⓑ Ⓒ Ⓓ		
16	Ⓐ Ⓑ Ⓒ Ⓓ	28	Ⓐ Ⓑ Ⓒ Ⓓ	40	Ⓐ Ⓑ Ⓒ Ⓓ	52	Ⓐ Ⓑ Ⓒ Ⓓ		
17	Ⓐ Ⓑ Ⓒ Ⓓ	29	Ⓐ Ⓑ Ⓒ Ⓓ	41	Ⓐ Ⓑ Ⓒ Ⓓ	53	Ⓐ Ⓑ Ⓒ Ⓓ		

1) In the figure below, what is the value of x?

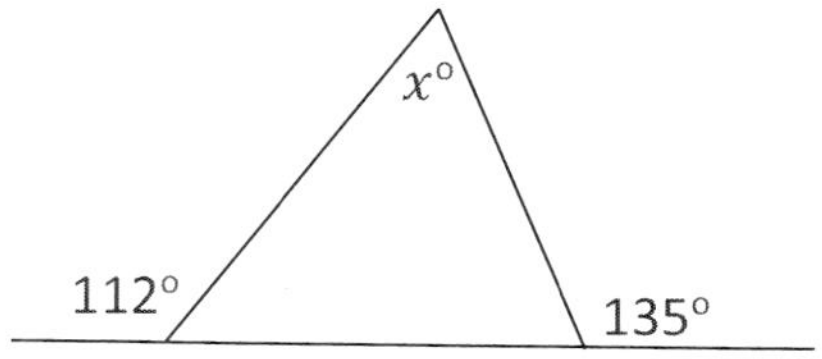

2) In the following right triangle, if the sides AB and BC become twice longer, what will be the ratio of the perimeter of the triangle to its area?

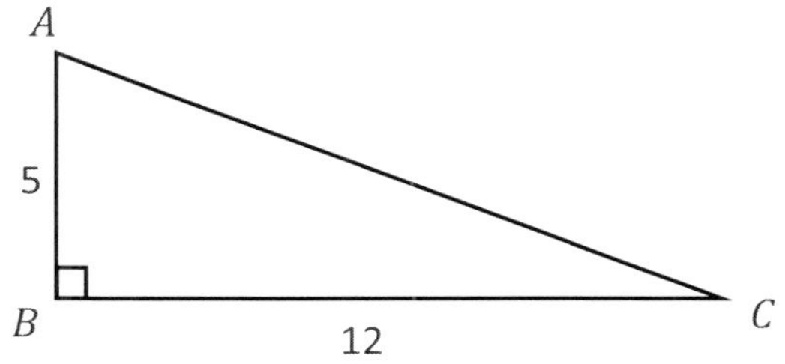

3) $-18 + 6 \times (-5) - [4 + 22 \times (-4)] \div 2 + 8 = ?$

4) If $\frac{x-3}{5} = N$ and $N = 6$, what is the value of x?

5) A construction company is building a wall. The company can build **30** cm of the wall per minute. After **40** minutes $\frac{3}{4}$ of the wall is completed. How many meters is the wall?

6) When a number is subtracted from **24** and the difference is divided by that number, the result is **3**. What is the number?

A. 2

B. 4

C. 6

D. 12

7) An angle is equal to one ninth of its supplement. What is the measure of that angle?

A. 18

B. 24

C. 36

D. 45

8) John traveled **150** km in **6** hours and Alice traveled **180** km in **4** hours. What is the ratio of the average speed of John to average speed of Alice?

A. 3: 2

B. 2: 3

C. 5: 9

D. 5: 6

9) If the area of the following rectangular $ABCD$ is **100**, and E is the midpoint of AB, what is the area of the shaded part?

A. 25

B. 50

C. 75

D. 80

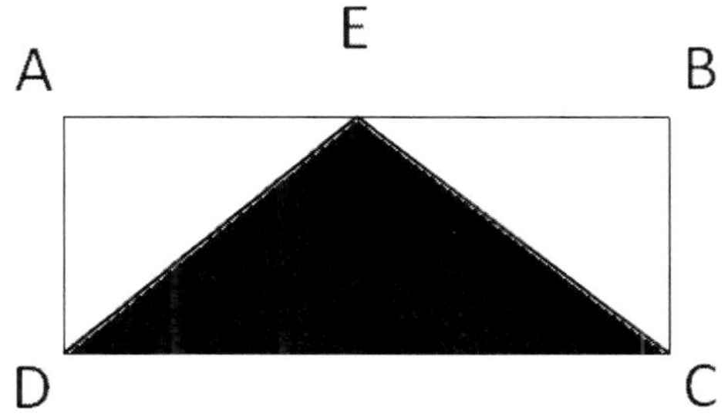

10)A taxi driver earns $\$9$ per $1-$hour work. If he works $\mathbf{10}$ hours a day and in $\mathbf{1}$ hour he uses $\mathbf{2}$ $-$liters petrol with price $\$\mathbf{1}$ for $\mathbf{1}$ $-$liter, how much money does he earn in one day?

A. $90
B. $88
C. $70
D. $60

Use the chart below to answer the question. The table below shows the number of different color marbles in a bag.

Color	Number of marbles
White	20
Black	30
Beige	40

11)There are also purple marbles in the bag. Which of the following can NOT be the probability of randomly selecting a purple marble from the bag?

A. $\frac{1}{10}$
B. $\frac{1}{4}$
C. $\frac{2}{5}$
D. $\frac{7}{15}$

12)Find the average of the following numbers: $\mathbf{17, 13, 7, 21, 22}$

A. 17
B. 16.5
C. 16
D. 11

13) The sum of six different negative integers is -70. If the smallest of these integers is -15, what is the largest possible value of one of the other five integers?

A. -14

B. -10

C. -5

D. -1

14) If $3x - 5 = 8.5$, what is the value of $5x + 3$?

A. 13

B. 15.5

C. 20.5

D. 25.5

15) The price of a sofa is decreased by 15% to $\$476$. What was its original price?

A. $480

B. $520

C. $560

D. $600

16) Right triangle ABC has two legs of lengths $9\ cm$ (AB) and $12\ cm$ (AC). What is the length of the third side (BC)?

A. $6\ cm$

B. $8\ cm$

C. $14\ cm$

D. $15\ cm$

Questions 17 to 19 are based on the following data

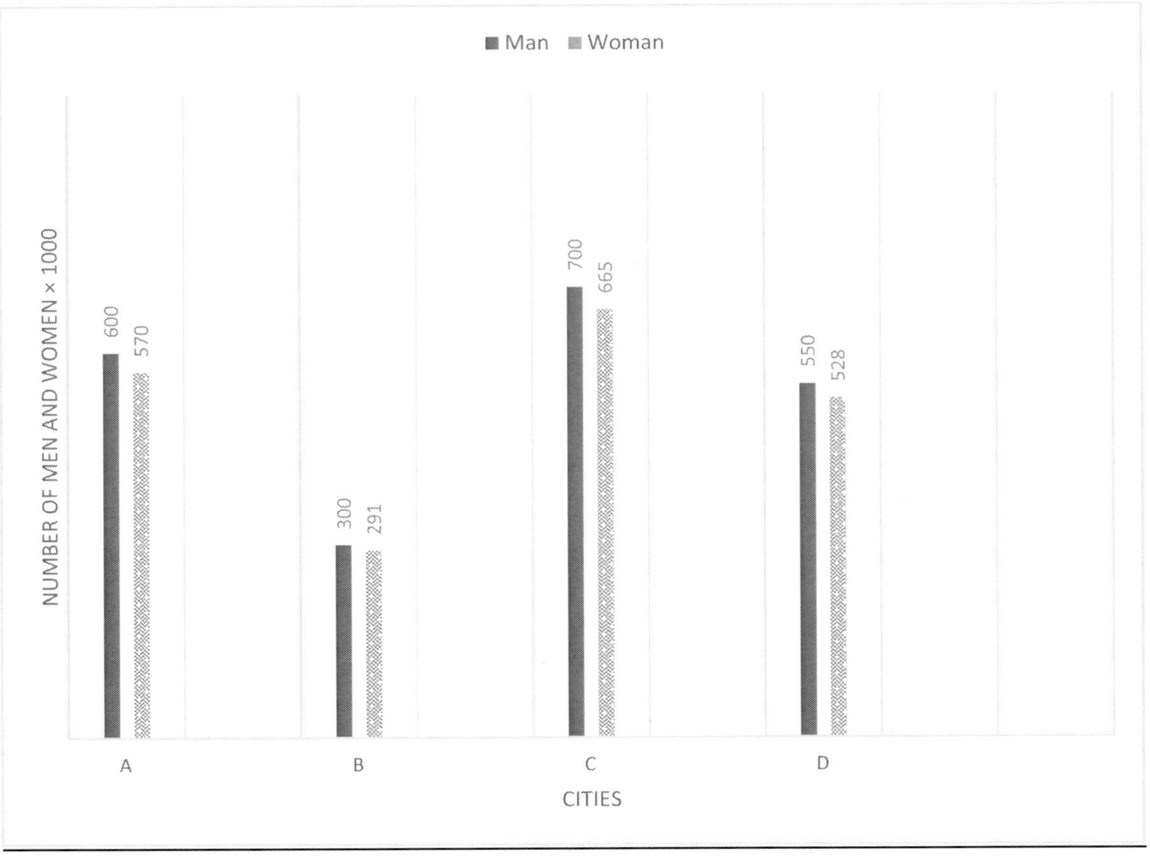

17) What's the maximum ratio of woman to man in the four cities?

A. 0.98

B. 0.97

C. 0.96

D. 0.95

18) What's the ratio of percentage of men in city ***A*** to percentage of women in city ***C***?

A. 0.9

B. 0.95

C. 1

D. 1.05

19) How many women should be added to city D until the ratio of women to men will be 1.2?

A. 120

B. 128

C. 132

D. 160

20) If 40% of a class are girls, and 25% of girls play tennis, what percent of the class play tennis?

A. 10%

B. 15%

C. 20%

D. 40%

21) The area of a circle is less than 64π. Which of the following can be the circumference of the circle? (Select one or more answer choices)

A. 12π

B. 16π

C. 24π

D. 32π

22) Which of the following values for x and y satisfy the following system of equations?

$$\begin{cases} x + 4y = 10 \\ 5x + 10y = 20 \end{cases}$$

A. $x = 3, y = 2$

B. $x = 2, y - 3$

C. $x = -2, y = 3$

D. $x = 3, y = -2$

23) If **60%** of A is 20% of B, then B is what percent of A?

A. 3%

B. 30%

C. 200%

D. 300%

24) In the following figure, **MN** is $\mathbf{40\ cm}$. How long is **ON**?

A. 25 cm

B. 20 cm

C. 15 cm

D. 10 cm

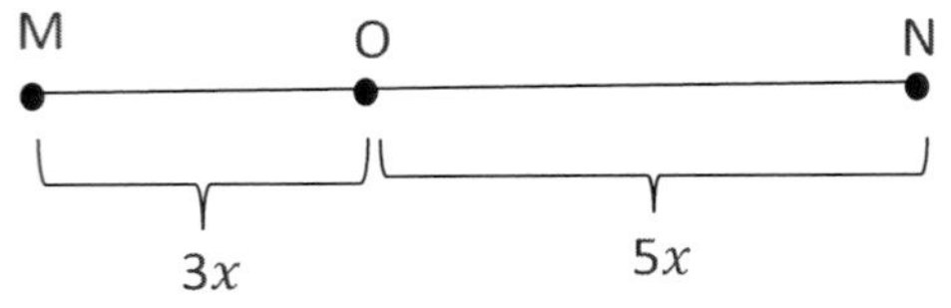

25) The price of a car was $\mathbf{\$20,000}$ in 2014, $\mathbf{\$16,000}$ in 2015 and $\mathbf{\$12,800}$ in 2016. What is the rate of depreciation of the price of the car per year?

A. 15%

B. 20%

C. 25%

D. 30%

26) The width of a box is one third of its length. The height of the box is one third of its width. If the length of the box is $\mathbf{27\ cm}$, what is the volume of the box?

A. 81 cm^3

B. 162 cm^3

C. 243 cm^3

D. 729 cm^3

27) How many possible outfit combinations come from six shirts, three slacks, and five ties?

A. 15

B. 18

C. 30

D. 90

28) A bank is offering 4.5% simple interest on a savings account. If you deposit $\$8,000$, how much interest will you earn in five years?

A. $360

B. $720

C. $1,800

D. $3,600

Gender	Under 45	45 or older	total
Male	12	6	18
Female	5	7	12
Total	17	13	30

29) The table above shows the distribution of age and gender for **30** employees in a company. If one employee is selected at random, what is the probability that the employee selected be either a female under age **45** or a male age **45** or older?

A. $\frac{5}{6}$

B. $\frac{5}{30}$

C. $\frac{6}{30}$

D. $\frac{11}{30}$

30)The cost, in thousands of dollars, of producing x thousands of textbooks is $C(x) = x^2 + 2x$. The revenue, also in thousands of dollars, is $R(x) = 40x$. Find the profit or loss if 30 textbooks are produced. (Profit = revenue – cost)

A. \$2,160 *profit*

B. \$240 *profit*

C. \$2,160 *loss*

D. \$240 *loss*

31)What is the length of **AB** in the following figure if $\mathbf{AE} = \mathbf{4}$, $\mathbf{CD} = \mathbf{6}$ and $\mathbf{AC} = \mathbf{12}$?

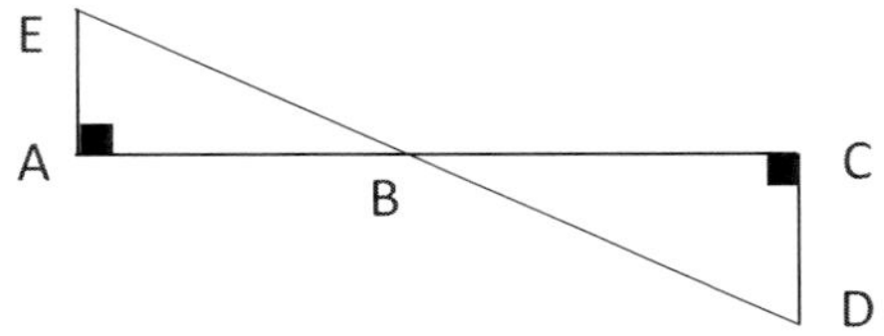

A. 3.8

B. 4.8

C. 7.2

D. 24

32)If the area of the following trapezoid is **126** cm, what is the perimeter of the trapezoid? (Figure not drawn to scale.)

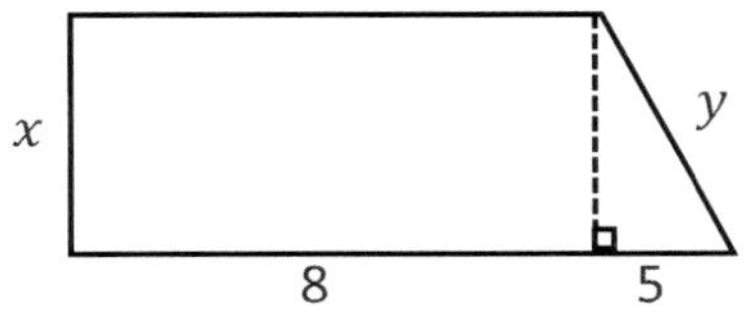

A. 12 *cm*

B. 32 *cm*

C. 46 *cm*

D. 55 *cm*

33)In five successive hours, a car traveled $\mathbf{40}$ ***km***, $\mathbf{45}$ ***km***, $\mathbf{50}$ ***km***, $\mathbf{35}$ ***km*** and $\mathbf{55}$ ***km***. In the next five hours, it traveled with an average speed of $\mathbf{50}$ ***km*** per hour. Find the total distance the car traveled in **10** hours.

A. 425 *km*

B. 450 *km*

C. 475 *km*

D. 500 *km*

34) How long does a **420**–miles trip take moving at **50 *miles per hour*** (mph)?

A. 4 *hours*

B. 6 *hours and* 24 *minutes*

C. 8 *hours and* 24 *minutes*

D. 8 *hours and* 30 *minutes*

35) If **5 *inches*** on a map represents an actual distance of **100** feet, then, what actual distance does **18** inches on the map represent?

A. 18

B. 100

C. 250

D. 360

36) Two third of **18** is equal to $\frac{2}{5}$ of what number?

A. 12

B. 20

C. 30

D. 60

37) The marked price of a computer is ***D*** dollar. Its price decreased by **20**% in January and later increased by **10**% in February. What is the final price of the computer in ***D*** dollar?

A. $0.80D$

B. $0.88D$

C. $0.90D$

D. $1.20D$

38) A $**40** shirt now selling for $**28** is discounted by what percent?

A. 20%

B. 30%

C. 40%

D. 60%

39) Which of the following could be the product of two consecutive prime numbers?

A. *A.* 2

B. *B.* 10

C. *C.* 14

D. *D.* 15

40) Which of the following lists shows the fractions in order from least to greatest?

$$\frac{3}{4}, \frac{2}{7}, \frac{3}{8}, \frac{5}{11}$$

A. $\frac{3}{8}, \frac{2}{7}, \frac{3}{4}, \frac{5}{11}$

B. $\frac{2}{7}, \frac{5}{11}, \frac{3}{8}, \frac{3}{4}$

C. $\frac{2}{7}, \frac{3}{8}, \frac{5}{11}, \frac{3}{4}$

D. $\frac{3}{8}, \frac{2}{7}, \frac{5}{11}, \frac{3}{4}$

41) A boat sails **40** miles south and then **30** miles east. How far is the boat from its start point?

A. 45 *miles*

B. 50 *miles*

C. 60 *miles*

D. 70 *miles*

42) The ratio of boys and girls in a class is **4**: **7**. If there are **44** students in the class, how many more boys should be enrolled to make the ratio of boys and girls **1**: **1**?

A. 8

B. 10

C. 12

D. 16

43) Sophia purchased a sofa for $\$530.40$. The sofa is regularly priced at $\$624$. What was the percent discount Sophia received on the sofa?

A. 12%

B. 15%

C. 20%

D. 25%

44) The score of Emma was half as that of Ava and the score of Mia was twice that of Ava. If the score of Mia was 60, what is the score of Emma?

A. 12

B. 15

C. 20

D. 30

45) A bag contains 18 balls: two green, five black, eight blue, a brown, a red and one white. If 17 balls are removed from the bag at random, what is the probability that a brown ball has been removed?

A. $\frac{1}{9}$

B. $\frac{1}{6}$

C. $\frac{16}{17}$

D. $\frac{17}{18}$

46) The average of five consecutive numbers is 38. What is the smallest number?

A. 38

B. 36

C. 34

D. 12

47) How many tiles of $8\ cm^2$ is needed to cover a floor of dimension $6\ cm$ by $24\ cm$?

A. 6

B. 12

C. 18

D. 24

48) The following graph shows the mark of seven students in mathematics. What is the mean (average) of the marks?

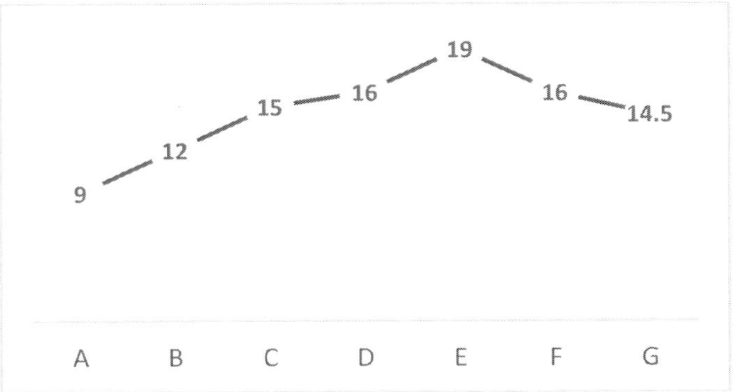

A. 15

B. 14.5

C. 14

D. 13.5

49) How many $\frac{1}{5}$ pound paperback books together weigh $\mathbf{50}$ pounds?

A. 25

B. 50

C. 150

D. 250

50) A rope weighs $\mathbf{600}$ ***grams*** per meter of length. What is the weight in kilograms of $\mathbf{12.2}$ meters of this rope? ($\mathbf{1}$ kilograms = $\mathbf{1000}$ grams)

A. 0.0732

B. 0.732

C. 7.32

D. 73.20

51)A chemical solution contains **4**% alcohol. If there is **24** ***ml*** of alcohol, what is the volume of the solution?

A. 240 ml

B. 480 ml

C. 600 ml

D. 1,200 ml

52)What is the volume of the following square pyramid?

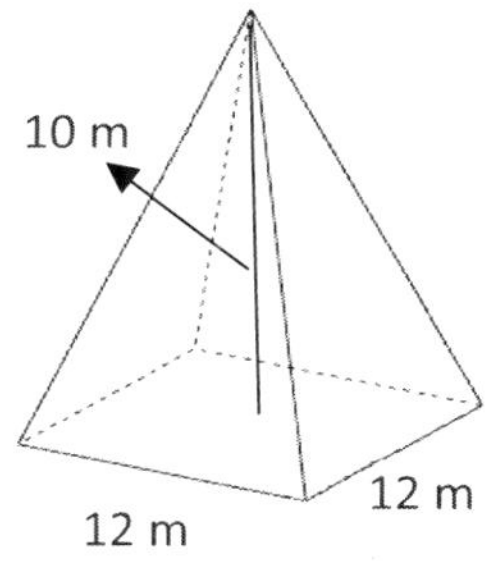

A. 120 m^3

B. 144 m^3

C. 480 m^3

D. 1440 $m3$

53)The average weight of **18** girls in a class is **60** ***kg*** and the average weight of **32** boys in the same class is **62** ***kg***. What is the average weight of all the **50** students in that class?

A. 60 kg

B. 61.28 kg

C. 61.68 kg

D. 62.90 kg

54)The price of a laptop is decreased by **10**% to $**360**. What is its original price?

A. $320

B. $380

C. $400

D. $450

55)What is the median of these numbers? **4, 9, 13, 8, 15, 18, 5**

A. 8

B. 9

C. 13

D. 15

56)The surface area of a cylinder is $\mathbf{150\pi\ cm^2}$. If its height is $\mathbf{10\ cm}$, what is the radius of the cylinder?

A. 13 cm

B. 11 cm

C. 15 cm

D. 5 cm

57)In 1999, the average worker's income increased $\mathbf{\$2,000}$ per year starting from $\mathbf{\$24,000}$ annual salary. Which equation represents income greater than average? (***I*** = income,
x = number of years after 1999)

A. $I > 2000x + 24000$

B. $I > -2000x + 24000$

C. $I < -2000x + 24000$

D. $I < 2000x - 24000$

IF YOU FINISH BEFORE TIME IS CALLED, YOU MAY CHECK YOUR WORK ON THIS TEST.

STOP

SHSAT Mathematics
Practice Test 2

2022

Total number of questions: 57

Total time for two parts: 75 Minutes

You may NOT use a calculator on this Test.

SHSAT Practice Tests Answer Sheet

Remove (or photocopy) these answer sheets and use them to complete the practice tests.

SHSAT Practice Test 2: Grid-ins Questions Answer Sheet

1

2

3

4

5

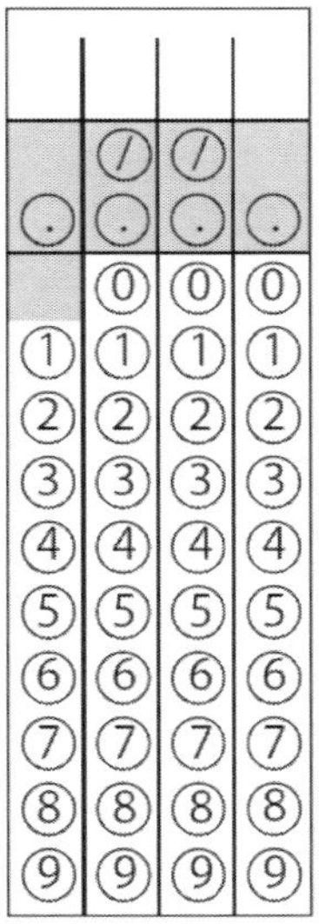

SHSAT Practice Test 2 – Multiple Choice Questions Answer Sheet

6	Ⓐ Ⓑ Ⓒ Ⓓ	18	Ⓐ Ⓑ Ⓒ Ⓓ	30	Ⓐ Ⓑ Ⓒ Ⓓ	42	Ⓐ Ⓑ Ⓒ Ⓓ	54	Ⓐ Ⓑ Ⓒ Ⓓ
7	Ⓐ Ⓑ Ⓒ Ⓓ	19	Ⓐ Ⓑ Ⓒ Ⓓ	31	Ⓐ Ⓑ Ⓒ Ⓓ	43	Ⓐ Ⓑ Ⓒ Ⓓ	55	Ⓐ Ⓑ Ⓒ Ⓓ
8	Ⓐ Ⓑ Ⓒ Ⓓ	20	Ⓐ Ⓑ Ⓒ Ⓓ	32	Ⓐ Ⓑ Ⓒ Ⓓ	44	Ⓐ Ⓑ Ⓒ Ⓓ	56	Ⓐ Ⓑ Ⓒ Ⓓ
9	Ⓐ Ⓑ Ⓒ Ⓓ	21	Ⓐ Ⓑ Ⓒ Ⓓ	33	Ⓐ Ⓑ Ⓒ Ⓓ	45	Ⓐ Ⓑ Ⓒ Ⓓ	57	Ⓐ Ⓑ Ⓒ Ⓓ
10	Ⓐ Ⓑ Ⓒ Ⓓ	22	Ⓐ Ⓑ Ⓒ Ⓓ	34	Ⓐ Ⓑ Ⓒ Ⓓ	46	Ⓐ Ⓑ Ⓒ Ⓓ		
11	Ⓐ Ⓑ Ⓒ Ⓓ	23	Ⓐ Ⓑ Ⓒ Ⓓ	35	Ⓐ Ⓑ Ⓒ Ⓓ	47	Ⓐ Ⓑ Ⓒ Ⓓ		
12	Ⓐ Ⓑ Ⓒ Ⓓ	24	Ⓐ Ⓑ Ⓒ Ⓓ	36	Ⓐ Ⓑ Ⓒ Ⓓ	48	Ⓐ Ⓑ Ⓒ Ⓓ		
13	Ⓐ Ⓑ Ⓒ Ⓓ	25	Ⓐ Ⓑ Ⓒ Ⓓ	37	Ⓐ Ⓑ Ⓒ Ⓓ	49	Ⓐ Ⓑ Ⓒ Ⓓ		
14	Ⓐ Ⓑ Ⓒ Ⓓ	26	Ⓐ Ⓑ Ⓒ Ⓓ	38	Ⓐ Ⓑ Ⓒ Ⓓ	50	Ⓐ Ⓑ Ⓒ Ⓓ		
15	Ⓐ Ⓑ Ⓒ Ⓓ	27	Ⓐ Ⓑ Ⓒ Ⓓ	39	Ⓐ Ⓑ Ⓒ Ⓓ	51	Ⓐ Ⓑ Ⓒ Ⓓ		
16	Ⓐ Ⓑ Ⓒ Ⓓ	28	Ⓐ Ⓑ Ⓒ Ⓓ	40	Ⓐ Ⓑ Ⓒ Ⓓ	52	Ⓐ Ⓑ Ⓒ Ⓓ		
17	Ⓐ Ⓑ Ⓒ Ⓓ	29	Ⓐ Ⓑ Ⓒ Ⓓ	41	Ⓐ Ⓑ Ⓒ Ⓓ	53	Ⓐ Ⓑ Ⓒ Ⓓ		

1) In the following shape, the area of the circle is 16π. What is the area of the square?

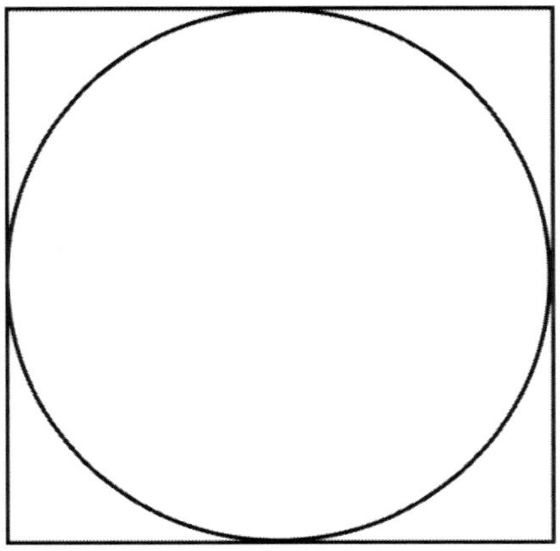

2) List A consists of the numbers $\{1, 3, 8, 10, 15\}$, and list B consists of the numbers $\{4, 6, 12, 14, 17\}$.

   If the two lists are combined, what is the median of the combined list?

3) A tree **32** feet tall casts a shadow **12** feet long. Jack is **6** feet tall. How long is Jack's shadow?

4) What is the value of the expression $\mathbf{3(x-2y)+(2-x)^2}$ when $\mathbf{x=5}$ and $=\mathbf{-3}$?

5) What is the value of $\mathbf{x}$ in the following equation? $\mathbf{-60=115-x}$

6) What's the area of the non-shaded part of the following figure?

A. 192

B. 152

C. 40

D. 42

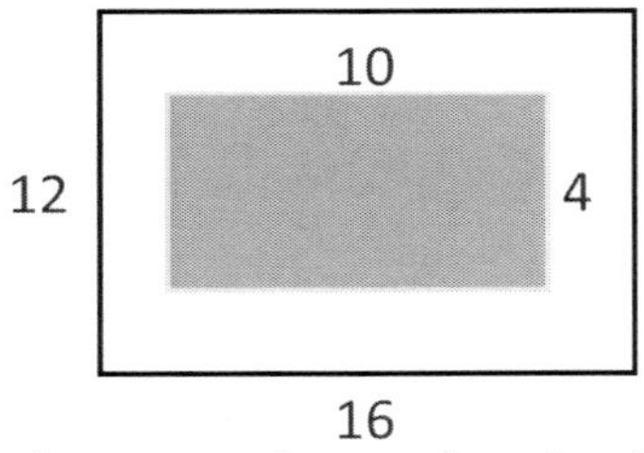

7) In the triangle below, if the measure of angle $\boldsymbol{A}$ is $\mathbf{37}$ degrees, then what is the value of $\boldsymbol{y}$? (figure is NOT drawn to scale)

A. 62

B. 70

C. 78

D. 86

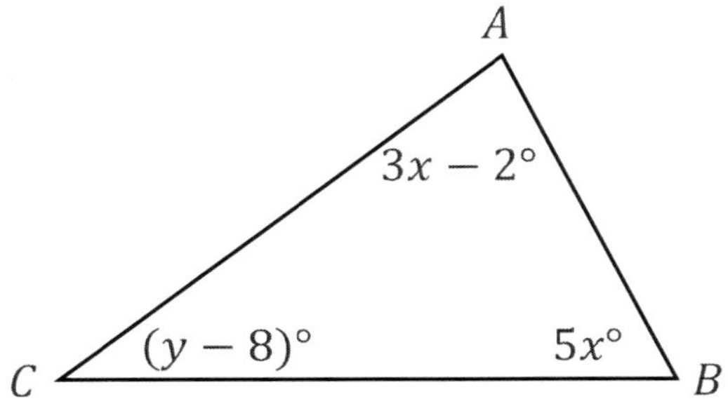

8) Simplify the expression.

$$(6x^3 - 8x^2 + 2x^4) - (4x^2 - 2x^4 + 2x^3)$$

A. $4x^4 + 4x^3 - 12x^2$

B. $4x^3 - 12x^2$

C. $4x^4 + 4x^3 - 12x^2$

D. $8x^3 - 12x^2$

<u>**Questions 9 and 11 are based on the following data**</u>

Types of air pollutions in 10 cities of a country

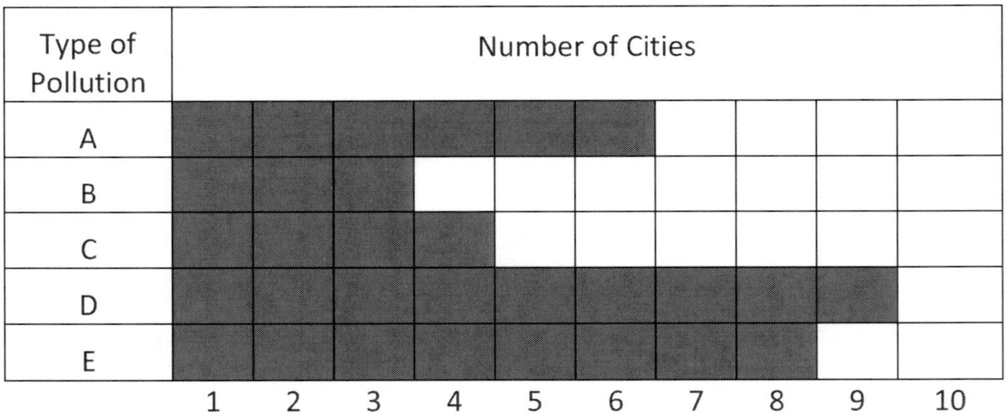

9) If $\boldsymbol{a}$ is the mean (average) of the number of cities in each pollution type category, $\boldsymbol{b}$ is the mode, and $\boldsymbol{c}$ is the median of the number of cities in each pollution type category, then which of the following must be true?

A. $a < b < c$

B. $b < a < c$

C. $a = c$

D. $b < c = a$

10) What percent of cities are in the type of pollution A, C, and E respectively?

A. $60\%, 40\%, 90\%$

B. $30\%, 40\%, 90\%$

C. $30\%, 40\%, 60\%$

D. $40\%, 60\%, 90\%$

11) How many cities should be added to type of pollutions $\boldsymbol{B}$ until the ratio of cities in type of pollution $\boldsymbol{B}$ to cities in type of pollution $\boldsymbol{E}$ will be $\mathbf{0.625}$?

A. 2

B. 3

C. 4

D. 5

12) There are only red and blue cards in a box. The probability of choosing a red card in the box at random is one third. If there are $\mathbf{246}$ blue cards, how many cards are in the box?

A. 123

B. 308

C. 328

D. 369

13) $\frac{1}{6b^2} + \frac{1}{6b} = \frac{1}{b^2}$, then b = ?

A. $-\frac{16}{15}$

B. 5

C. $-\frac{15}{16}$

D. 8

14) In two successive years, the population of a town is increased by **15%** and **20%**. What percent of the population is increased after two years?

A. 32%

B. 35%

C. 38%

D. 68%

15) Which of the following graphs represents the compound inequality $-2 \leq 2x - 4 < 8$?

A.

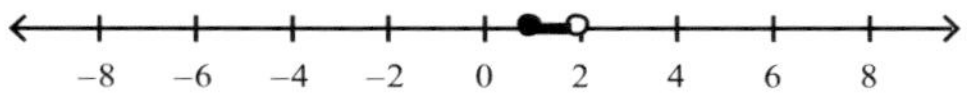

B.

C.

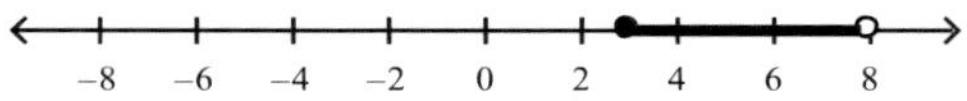

D.

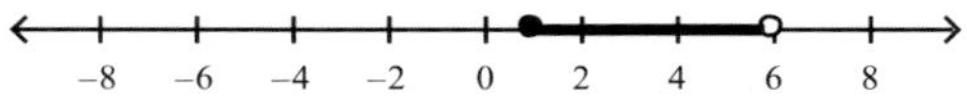

16) What is the volume of a box with the following dimensions?

Height = 4 cm Width = 5 cm Length = 6 cm

A. 15 cm^3

B. 60 cm^3

C. 90 cm^3

D. 120 cm^3

17) In the diagram below, circle $\boldsymbol{A}$ represents the set of all odd numbers, circle $\boldsymbol{B}$ represents the set of all negative numbers, and circle $\boldsymbol{C}$ represents the set of all multiples of **5**. Which number could be replaced with $\boldsymbol{y}$?

A. 5

B. 0

C. -5

D. -10

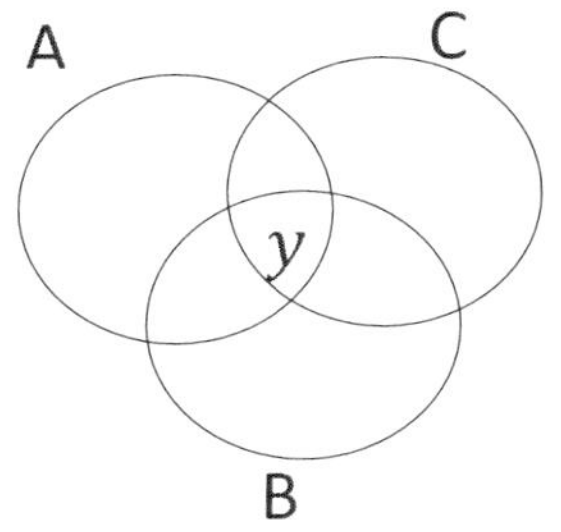

18) A basket contains **20** balls and the average weight of each of these balls is **25** $\boldsymbol{g}$. The five heaviest balls have an average weight of **40** $\boldsymbol{g}$ each. If we remove the five heaviest balls from the basket, what is the average weight of the remaining balls?

A. 10

B. 20

C. 30

D. 35

19) Mr. Carlos family are choosing a menu for their reception. They have **3** choices of appetizers, **5** choices of entrees, **4** choices of cake. How many different menu combinations are possible for them to choose?

A. 12

B. 32

C. 60

D. 120

20) In a stadium the ratio of home fans to visiting fans in a crowd is $\mathbf{5:7}$. Which of the following could be the total number of fans in the stadium?

A. 12,324

B. 42,326

C. 44,566

D. 66,812

21) Last week $\mathbf{24,000}$ fans attended a football match. This week three times as many bought tickets, but one sixth of them cancelled their tickets. How many are attending this week?

A. 48,000

B. 54,000

C. 60,000

D. 72,000

22) What is the perimeter of a square in centimeters that has an area of $\mathbf{595.36}\ \boldsymbol{cm^2}$?

A. 97.6

B. 96.2

C. 95.7

D. 92.6

23) A bread recipe calls for $\mathbf{2\frac{2}{3}}$ cups of flour. If you only have $\mathbf{2\frac{5}{6}}$ cups, how much more flour is needed?

A. 1

B. $\frac{1}{2}$

C. 2

D. $\frac{5}{6}$

24)The perimeter of a rectangular yard is **60** meters. What is its length if its width is twice its length?

A. 10 meters

B. 18 meters

C. 20 meters

D. 24 meters

25)Which of the following shows the numbers in increasing order?

$$\frac{2}{3},\ 0.68,\ 67\%,\ \frac{4}{5}$$

A. $67\%, 0.68, \frac{2}{3}, \frac{4}{5}$

B. $67\%, 0.68, \frac{4}{5}, \frac{2}{3}$

C. $0.68, 67\%, \frac{2}{3}, \frac{4}{5}$

D. $\frac{2}{3}, 67\%, 0.68, \frac{4}{5}$

26)The mean of **50** test scores was calculated as **88**. But, it turned out that one of the scores was misread as **94** but it was **69**. What is the correct mean of the test scores?

A. 85

B. 87

C. 87.5

D. 88.5

27) If Jim adds **100** stamps to his current stamp collection, the total number of stamps will be equal to $\frac{6}{5}$ the current number of stamps. If Jim adds **50%** more stamps to the current collection, how many stamps will be in the collection?

A. 150

B. 300

C. 600

D. 750

28) Two dice are thrown simultaneously, what is the probability of getting a sum of **6** or **9**?

A. $\frac{1}{3}$

B. $\frac{1}{4}$

C. $\frac{1}{6}$

D. $\frac{1}{12}$

29) A swimming pool holds **2,000** cubic feet of water. The swimming pool is **25** feet long and **10** feet wide. How deep is the swimming pool?

A. 2
B. 4
C. 6
D. 8

30) What is the area of a square whose diagonal is **8**?

A. 16
B. 32
C. 36
D. 64

31) The sum of **8** numbers is greater than **240** and less than **320**. Which of the following could be the average (arithmetic mean) of the numbers?

A. 30

B. 35

C. 40

D. 45

32) Anita's trick–or–treat bag contains **12** pieces of chocolate, **18** suckers, **18** pieces of gum and **24** pieces of licorice. If she randomly pulls a piece of candy from her bag, what is the probability of her pulling out a piece of sucker?

A. $\frac{1}{3}$

B. $\frac{1}{4}$

C. $\frac{1}{6}$

D. $\frac{1}{12}$

33) The average of **6** numbers is **12**. The average of **4** of those numbers is **10**. What is the average of the other two numbers?

A. 10

B. 12

C. 14

D. 16

34) In the following figure, point Q lies on line n, what is the value of y if $x = 35$?

A. 15

B. 25

C. 35

D. 45

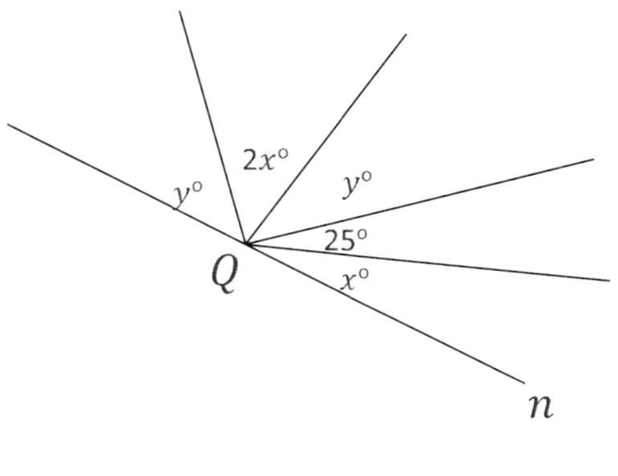

35)The perimeter of the trapezoid below (not drawn to scale) is **36 *cm***. What is its area?

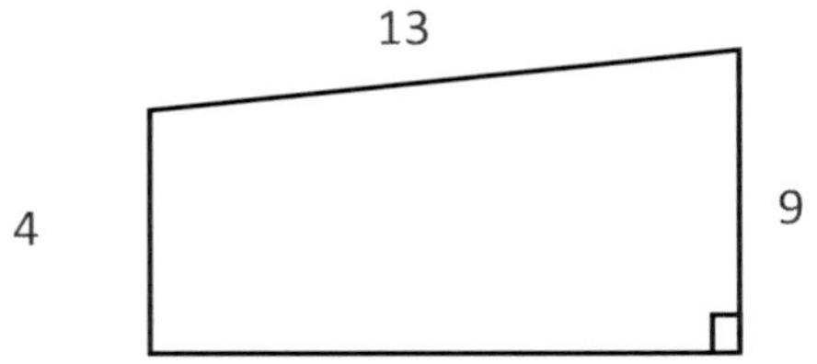

A. $576\ cm^2$

B. $78\ cm^2$

C. $48\ cm^2$

D. $24\ cm^2$

36)If **150**% of a number is **75**, then what is the **90**% of that number?

A. 45

B. 50

C. 70

D. 85

37)Triangle ABC is similar to triangle ADE. What is the length of side EC?

A. 4

B. 9

C. 18

D. 4.5

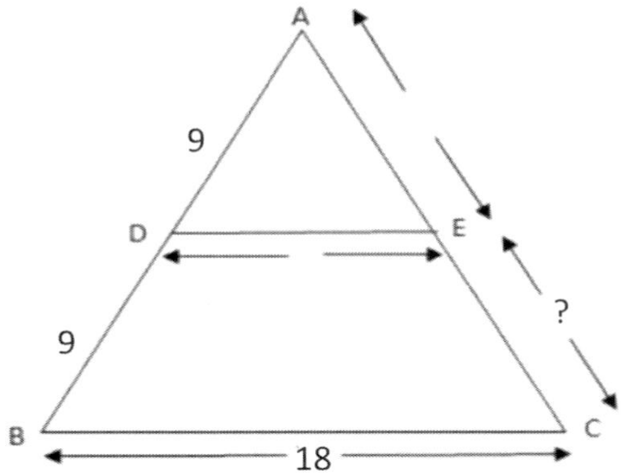

38)A football team had **$20,000** to spend on supplies. The team spent **$14,000** on new balls. New sport shoes cost **$120** each. Which of the following inequalities represent the number of new shoes the team can purchase?

A. $120x + 14{,}000 \leq 20{,}000$

B. $120x + 14{,}000 \geq 20{,}000$

C. $14{,}000x + 120 \leq 20{,}000$

D. $14{,}000x + 120 \geq 20{,}000$

39) A card is drawn at random from a standard **52**–card deck, what is the probability that the card is of Hearts? (The deck includes **13** of each suit clubs, diamonds, hearts, and spades)

A. $\frac{1}{3}$

B. $\frac{1}{4}$

C. $\frac{1}{6}$

D. $\frac{1}{52}$

40) The average of five numbers is **24**. If a sixth number that is greater than **42** is added, then, which of the following could be the new average? (Select one or more answer choices)

A. 25

B. 26

C. 27

D. 28

41) Ella (***E***) is **4** years older than her friend Ava (***A***) who is **3** years younger than her sister Sofia (***S***). If ***E***, ***A*** and ***S*** denote their ages, which one of the following represents the given information?

A. $\begin{cases} E = A + 4 \\ S = A - 3 \end{cases}$

B. $\begin{cases} E = A + 4 \\ A = S + 3 \end{cases}$

C. $\begin{cases} A = E + 4 \\ S = A - 3 \end{cases}$

D. $\begin{cases} E = A + 4 \\ A = S - 3 \end{cases}$

42)The length of a rectangle is 3 meters greater than 4 times its width. The perimeter of the rectangle is 36 meters. What is the area of the rectangle in meters?

A. 35

B. 45

C. 55

D. 65

43)The ratio of boys and girls in a class is $4:7$. If there are 44 students in the class, how many more boys should be enrolled to make the ratio $1:1$?

A. 8

B. 10

C. 12

D. 14

44)Mr. Jones saves $\$2,500$ out of his monthly family income of $\$55,000$. What fractional part of his income does he save?

A. $\frac{1}{22}$

B. $\frac{1}{11}$

C. $\frac{3}{25}$

D. $\frac{2}{15}$

45)Jason needs an 75% average in his writing class to pass. On his first 4 exams, he earned scores of $68\%, 72\%, 85\%$, and 90%. What is the minimum score Jason can earn on his fifth and final test to pass?

A. 375

B. 315

C. 90

D. 60

46) What is the value of x in the following equation?

$$\frac{2}{3}x + \frac{1}{6} = \frac{1}{3}$$

A. 6

B. $\frac{1}{2}$

C. $\frac{1}{3}$

D. $\frac{1}{4}$

47) What is the surface area of the cylinder below?

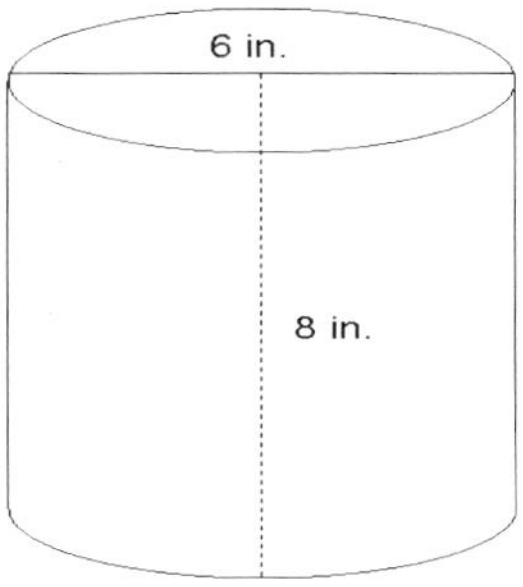

A. $48\pi\ in^2$

B. $57\pi\ in^2$

C. $66\pi\ in^2$

D. $288\pi\ in^2$

48) The square of a number is $\frac{25}{64}$. What is the cube of that number?

A. $\frac{5}{8}$

B. $\frac{25}{254}$

C. $\frac{125}{512}$

D. $\frac{125}{64}$

49) What is the median of these numbers? **2, 27, 28, 19, 67, 44, 35**

A. 19

B. 28

C. 44

D. 35

50) Right triangle ABC has two legs of length $6\ cm$ (AB) and $8\ cm$ (AC). What is the length of the third side (BC)?

A. $4\ cm$

B. $6\ cm$

C. $8\ cm$

D. $10\ cm$

51) What is the equivalent temperature of $104°F$ in Celsius? $C = \frac{5}{9}\ (F - 32)$

A. 32

B. 40

C. 48

D. 52

52) If 40% of a number is 4, what is the number?

A. 4

B. 8

C. 10

D. 12

53) The circle graph below shows all Mr. Green's expenses for last month. If he spent $\$660$ on his car, how much did he spend for his rent?

A. \$700

B. \$740

C. \$780

D. \$810

Mr. Green's monthly expenses

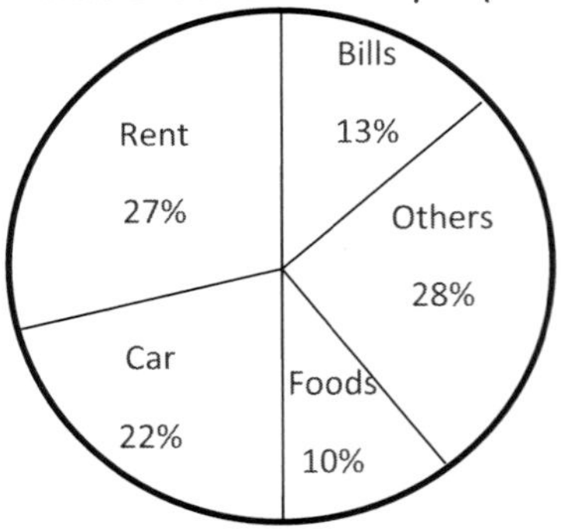

54) Jason is **9** miles ahead of Joe running at **5.5** miles per hour and Joe is running at the speed of **7** miles per hour. How long does it take Joe to catch Jason?

A. 3 hours

B. 4 hours

C. 6 hours

D. 8 hour

55) **55** Students took an exam and **11** of them failed. What percent of the students passed the exam?

A. 20%

B. 40%

C. 60%

D. 80%

56) A bank is offering **3.5%** simple interest on a savings account. If you deposit $**12,000**, how much interest will you earn in two years?

A. $420

B. $840

C. $4,200

D. $8,400

57) What is the area of the shaded region if the diameter of the bigger circle is **12** inches and the diameter of the smaller circle is **8** inches?

A. $16\pi\ in^2$

B. $20\pi\ in^2$

C. $36\pi\ in^2$

D. $80\pi\ in^2$

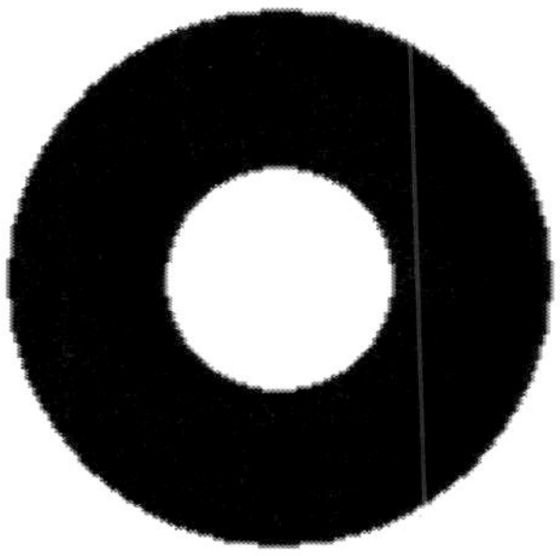

IF YOU FINISH BEFORE TIME IS CALLED, YOU MAY CHECK YOUR WORK ON THIS TEST.

STOP

SHSAT Mathematics Practice Tests Answer Keys

Now, it's time to review your results to see where you went wrong and what areas you need to improve.

SHSAT Mathematics Practice Tests Answer Key

SHSAT Practice Test 1

1	67	16	D	31	B	46	B
2	$\frac{1}{2}$	17	B	32	C	47	C
3	2	18	D	33	C	48	B
4	33	19	C	34	C	49	D
5	16	20	A	35	D	50	C
6	C	21	A	36	C	51	C
7	A	22	C	37	B	52	C
8	C	23	D	38	B	53	B
9	B	24	A	39	D	54	C
10	C	25	B	40	C	55	B
11	D	26	D	41	B	56	D
12	C	27	D	42	C	57	A
13	C	28	C	43	B		
14	D	29	D	44	B		
15	C	30	B	45	D		

SHSAT Practice Test 2

1	64	16	D	31	B	46	D
2	9	17	C	32	B	47	C
3	2.25	18	B	33	D	48	C
4	42	19	C	34	B	49	B
5	175	20	A	35	B	50	D
6	B	21	C	36	A	51	B
7	D	22	A	37	B	52	C
8	A	23	D	38	A	53	D
9	C	24	A	39	B	54	C
10	A	25	D	40	D	55	D
11	A	26	C	41	D	56	B
12	D	27	D	42	B	57	B
13	B	28	B	43	C		
14	C	29	D	44	A		
15	D	30	B	45	D		

SHSAT Mathematics Practice Tests Answers and Explanations

SHSAT Mathematics Practice Test 1

1) **The answer is 67**

First, find the angles α and β. Angles 112 and α are supplementary. Then:

$\alpha + 112 = 180 \rightarrow \alpha = 180° - 112° = 68°$

Angles 135 and β are also supplementary. $\beta = 180° - 135° = 45°$

The sum of all angles in a triangle is 180 degrees. Then:

$x + \alpha + \beta = 180° \rightarrow x = 180° - 68° - 45° = 67°$

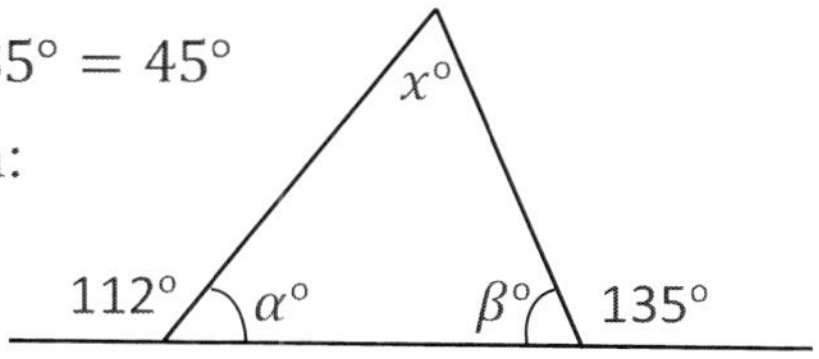

2) **The answer is $\frac{1}{2}$**

$AB = 5$ and $BC = 12$, $AC = \sqrt{12^2 + 5^2} = \sqrt{144 + 25} = \sqrt{169} = 13$

Perimeter $= 5 + 12 + 13 = 30$, Area $= \frac{5 \times 12}{2} = 5 \times 6 = 30$

In this case, the ratio of the perimeter of the triangle to its area is: $\frac{30}{30} = 1$

If the sides AB and BC become twice longer, then: $AB = 10$ And $BC = 24$

$AC = \sqrt{24^2 + 10^2} = \sqrt{576 + 100} = \sqrt{676} = 26$

Perimeter $= 26 + 24 + 10 = 60$, Area $= \frac{10 \times 24}{2} = 10 \times 12 = 120$

In this case the ratio of the perimeter of the triangle to its area is: $\frac{60}{120} = \frac{1}{2}$

3) **The answer is 2**

Use PEMDAS (order of operation):

$-18 + 6 \times (-5) - [4 + 22 \times (-4)] \div 2 + 8 = -18 - 30 - [4 - 88] \div 2 + 8$

$= -48 - [-84] \div 2 + 8 = -48 + 84 \div 2 + 8 = -48 + 42 + 8 = 2$

4) **The answer is 33**

Since $N = 6$, substitute 6 for N in the equation $\frac{x-3}{5} = N$, which gives $\frac{x-3}{5} = 6$. Multiplying both sides of $\frac{x-3}{5} = 6$ by 5 gives $x - 3 = 30$ *and* then adding 3 to both sides of $x - 3 = 30$ then, $x = 33$.

5) **The answer is 16**

The rate of construction company $= \frac{30\ cm}{1\ min} = 30 \frac{cm}{min}$

The height of the wall after 40 minutes $= \frac{30\ cm}{1\ min} \times 40\ min = 1{,}200\ cm$

Let x be the height of wall, then $\frac{3}{4}x = 1{,}200\ cm \rightarrow x = \frac{4\times1200}{3} \rightarrow x = 1{,}600\ cm =$ $16\ m$

6) **Choice C is correct**

Let x be the number. Write the equation and solve for x. $(24 - x) \div x = 3$
Multiply both sides by x. $(24 - x) = 3x$, then add x both sides. $24 = 4x$, now divide both sides by 4. $x = 6$

7) **Choice A is correct**

The sum of supplement angles is 180 degrees. Let x be that angle. Therefore, $x + 9x = 180 \rightarrow 10x = 180$, divide both sides by 10: $x = 18$

8) **Choice C is correct**

The average speed of john is: $150 \div 6 = 25\ km$
The average speed of Alice is: $180 \div 4 = 45\ km$
Write the ratio and simplify. $25:45 \Rightarrow 5:9$

9) **Choice B is correct**

Since, E is the midpoint of AB, then the area of all triangles DAE, DEF, CFE and CBE are equal. Let x be the area of one of the triangle, Then:
$4x = 100 \rightarrow x = 25$
The area of $DEC = 2x = 2(25) = 50$

10) **Choice C is correct**

$\$9 \times 10 = \$90$, Petrol use: $10 \times 2 = 20$ liters
Petrol cost: $20 \times \$1 = \$20$, Money earned: $\$90 - \$20 = \$70$

11) **Choice D is correct**

Let x be the number of purple marbles. Let's review the choices provided:
A. $\frac{1}{10}$, if the probability of choosing a purple marble is one out of ten, then:
Probability $= \frac{number\ of\ desired\ outcomes}{number\ of\ total\ outcomes} = \frac{x}{20+30+40+x} = \frac{1}{10}$
Use cross multiplication and solve for x. $10x = 90 + x \rightarrow 9x = 90 \rightarrow x = 9$

Since the number of purple marbles can be 9, then, choice A can be the probability of randomly selecting a purple marble from the bag. Use the same method for other choices.

B. $\frac{1}{4}$, $\frac{x}{20+30+40+x} = \frac{1}{4} \rightarrow 4x = 90 + x \rightarrow 3x = 90 \rightarrow x = 30$

C. $\frac{2}{5}$, $\frac{x}{20+30+40+x} = \frac{2}{5} \rightarrow 5x = 180 + 2x \rightarrow 3x = 180 \rightarrow x = 60$

D. $\frac{7}{15}$, $\frac{x}{20+30+40+x} = \frac{7}{15} \rightarrow 15x = 630 + 7x \rightarrow 8x = 630 \rightarrow x = 78.75$

Number of purple marbles cannot be a decimal. Therefore, Choice D can NOT be the probability of randomly selecting a purple marble from the bag.

12) **Choice C is correct**

Use the average formula: Average $= \frac{sum\ of\ terms}{number\ of\ terms} = \frac{17+13+7+21+22}{5} = \frac{80}{5} = 16$

13) **Choice C is correct**

The smallest number is -15. To find the largest possible value of one of the other five integers, we need to choose the smallest possible integers for four of them. Let x be the largest number. Then: $-70 = (-15) + (-14) + (-13) + (-12) + (-11) + x \rightarrow -70 = -65 + x \rightarrow x = -70 + 65 = -5$

14) **Choice D is correct.**

Solve for x: $3x - 5 = 8.5 \rightarrow 3x = 8.5 + 5 = 13.5 \rightarrow x = \frac{13.5}{3} = 4.5$

Then: $5x + 3 = 5\,(4.5) + 3 = 22.5 + 3 = 25.5$

15) **Choice C is correct**

Let x be the original price. If the price of the sofa is decreased by 15% to \$476, then: 85% of $x = 476 \Rightarrow 0.85x = 476 \Rightarrow x = \frac{476}{0.85} = 560$

16) **Choice D is correct**

Use Pythagorean Theorem: $a^2 + b^2 = c^2$

$92 + 122 = c^2 \Rightarrow 81 + 144 = c^2 \Rightarrow 225 = c^2 \Rightarrow c = 15$

17) **Choice B is correct**

Ratio of women to men in city A: $\frac{570}{600} = 0.95$

Ratio of women to men in city B: $\frac{291}{300} = 0.97$

Ratio of women to men in city C: $\frac{665}{700} = 0.95$

Ratio of women to men in city D: $\frac{528}{550} = 0.96$

Choice B is the maximum number.

18) **Choice D is correct**

Percentage of men in city $A = \frac{600}{1,170} \times 100 = 51.28\%$

Percentage of women in city $C = \frac{665}{1365} \times 100 = 48.72\%$

Percentage of men in city A to percentage of women in city $C = \frac{51.28}{48.72} = 1.05$

(Notice that $\frac{51.28}{48.72}$ is bigger than 1 and only choice D is bigger than 1)

19) **Choice C is correct**

Let the number of women should be added to city D be x, then:

$\frac{528 + x}{550} = 1.2 \rightarrow 528 + x = 550 \times 1.2 = 660 \rightarrow x = 132$

20) **Choice A is correct**

The percent of girls playing tennis is: $40\% \times 25\% = 0.40 \times 0.25 = 0.10 = 10\%$

21) **Choice A is correct**

Area of the circle is less than 16π. Use the formula of areas of circles.

Area $= \pi r^2 \Rightarrow 64\,\pi > \pi r^2 \Rightarrow 64 > r^2 \Rightarrow r < 8$

The radius of the circle is less than 8. Let's put 8 for the radius. Now, use the circumference formula: Circumference $= 2\pi r = 2\pi\,(8) = 16\,\pi$

Since the radius of the circle is less than 8. Then, the circumference of the circle must be less than 16π. Only choice A is less than 16π.

22) **Choice C is correct**

$\begin{cases} x + 4y = 10 \\ 5x + 10y = 20 \end{cases} \rightarrow$ Multiply the top equation by -5 then,

$\begin{cases} -5x - 20y = -50 \\ 5x + 10y = 20 \end{cases} \rightarrow$

Add two equations: $-10y = -30 \rightarrow y = 3$, plug in the value of y into the first equation

$x + 4y = 10 \rightarrow x + 4(3) = 10 \rightarrow x + 12 = 10$

Subtract 12 from both sides of the equation. Then: $x + 12 = 10 \rightarrow x = -2$

23) **Choice D is correct**

Write the equation and solve for B: $0.60A = 0.20B$, divide both sides by 0.20, then:

$\frac{0.60}{0.20} A = B$, therefore: $B = 3A$, and B is 3 times of A or it's 300% of A.

24) **Choice A is correct**

The length of MN is equal to: $3x + 5x = 8x$. Then: $8x = 40 \rightarrow x = \frac{40}{8} = 5$

The length of ON is equal to: $5x = 5 \times 5 = 25\ cm$

25) **Choice B is correct**

Use this formula: Percent of Change= $\frac{\text{New Value} - \text{Old Value}}{\text{Old Value}} \times 100\%$

$\frac{16000-20000}{20000} \times 100\% = 20\%$ and $\frac{12800-16000}{16000} \times 100\% = 20\%$

The rate of depreciation of the price of the car per year is 20%.

26) **Choice D is correct**

If the length of the box is 27, then the width of the box is one third of it, 9, and the height of the box is 3 (one third of the width). The volume of the box is: $V = lwh = (27)(9)(3) = 729$

27) **Choice D is correct**

To find the number of possible outfit combinations, multiply number of options for each factor: $6 \times 3 \times 5 = 90$

28) **Choice C is correct**

Use simple interest formula: $I = prt$ (I = Interest, p = principal, r = rate, t = time)

$I = (8{,}000)(0.045)(5) = 1{,}800$

29) **Choice D is correct**

Of the 30 employees, there are 5 females under age 45 and 6 males age 45 or older. Therefore, the probability that the person selected will be either a female under age 45 or a male age 45 or older is: $\frac{5}{30} + \frac{6}{30} = \frac{11}{30}$

30) **Choice B is correct**

Plug in the value of $x = 30$ into both equations. Then: $C(x) = x^2 + 2x = (30)^2 + 2(30) = 900 + 60 = 960$. $R(x) = 40x = 40 \times 30 = 1{,}200 \rightarrow 1{,}200 - 960 = 240$

The profit of producing 30 textbooks is $240.

31) **Choice B is correct**

Two triangles ΔBAE and ΔBCD are similar. Then:

$\frac{AE}{CD} = \frac{AB}{BC} \rightarrow \frac{4}{6} = \frac{x}{12} \rightarrow 48 - 4x = 6x \rightarrow 10x = 48 \rightarrow x = 4.8$

32) **Choice C is correct**

The area of the trapezoid is:

Area$= \frac{1}{2}h(b_1 + b_2) = \frac{1}{2}(x)(13 + 8) = 126 \rightarrow 10.5x = 126 \rightarrow x = 12$

$y = \sqrt{5^2 + 12^2} = \sqrt{25 + 144} = \sqrt{169} = 13$

The perimeter of the trapezoid is: $12 + 13 + 8 + 13 = 46$

33) **Choice C is correct**

Add the first 5 numbers. $40 + 45 + 50 + 35 + 55 = 225$

To find the distance traveled in the next 5 hours, multiply the average by number of hours.

$Distance = Average \times Rate = 50 \times 5 = 250$. Add both numbers. $250 + 225 = 475$

34) **Choice C is correct**

Use distance formula:

Distance=Rate×time⇒ $420 = 50 \times T$, divide both sides by 50. $\frac{420}{50} = T \Rightarrow T = 8.4$ hours.

Change hours to minutes for the decimal part. 0.4 hours $= 0.4 \times 60 = 24$ minutes.

35)**Choice D is correct**

First calculate the number of feet that 1 inch represents: $100\ ft \div 5\ in = 20\ ft/in$

Then multiply this by the total number of inches: $18\ in \times 20\ ft/in = 360\ ft$

36)**Choice C is correct**

Let x be the number. Write the equation and solve for x. $\frac{2}{3} \times 18 = \frac{2}{5}.\ x \Rightarrow \frac{2\times18}{3} = \frac{2x}{5}$, use cross multiplication to solve for x. $5 \times 36 = 2x \times 3 \Rightarrow 180 = 6x \Rightarrow x = 30$

37)**Choice B is correct**

To find the discount, multiply the number by (100% – rate of discount).

Therefore, for the first discount we get: $(D)(100\% - 20\%) = (D)(0.80) = 0.80\ D$

For increase of 10%: $(0.85D)(100\% + 10\%) = (0.85D)(1.10) = 0.88D = 88\%$ of D

38)**Choice B is correct**

Use the formula for Percent of Change:

$\frac{New\ Value - Old\ Value}{Old\ Value} \times 100\% \rightarrow \frac{28-40}{40} \times 100\% = -30\%$

(Negative sign here means that the new price is less than old price).

39)**Choices D is correct**

Some of prime numbers are: $2, 3, 5, 7, 11, 13$

Find the product of two consecutive prime numbers:

$2 \times 3 = 6$ (not in the options)

$3 \times 5 = 15$ (bingo!)

$5 \times 7 = 35$ (not in the options)

$7 \times 11 = 77$ (not in the options)

40)**Choice C is correct**

Let's compare each fraction: $\frac{2}{7} < \frac{3}{8} < \frac{5}{11} < \frac{3}{4}$

Only choice C provides the right order.

41) **Choice B is correct**

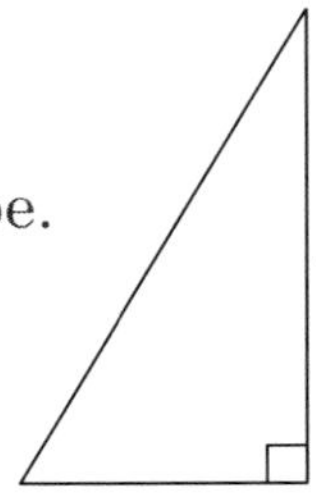

Use the information provided in the question to draw the shape.
Use Pythagorean Theorem: $a^2 + b^2 = c^2$
$40^2 + 30^2 = c^2 \Rightarrow 1600 + 900 = c^2 \Rightarrow 2500 = c^2 \Rightarrow c = 50$

42) **Choice C is correct**

The ratio of boy to girls is 4:7. Therefore, there are 4 boys out of 11 students. To find the answer, first divide the total number of students by 11, then multiply the result by 4.
$44 \div 11 = 4 \Rightarrow 4 \times 4 = 16$
There are 16 boys and 28 (44 – 16) girls. So, 12 more boys should be enrolled to make the ratio 1:1

43) **Choice B is correct**

$\frac{530.40}{624} = 0.85 = 85\%$, Since 530.40 is 85% of 624. Therefore, the discount is:
$100\% - 85\% = 15\%$

44) **Choice B is correct**

If the score of Mia was 60, therefore the score of Ava is 30. Since, the score of Emma was half as that of Ava, therefore, the score of Emma is 15.

45) **Choice D is correct**

If 17 balls are removed from the bag at random, there will be one ball in the bag.
The probability of choosing a brown ball is 1 out of 18. Therefore, the probability of not choosing a brown ball is 17 out of 18 and the probability of having not a brown ball after removing 17 balls is the same.

46) **Choice B is correct**

Let x be the smallest number. Then, these are the numbers: x, $x+1$, $x+2$, $x+3$, $x+4$
Average $= \frac{sum\ of\ terms}{number\ of\ terms} \Rightarrow 38 = \frac{x+(x+1)+(x+2)+(x+3)+(x+4)}{5} \Rightarrow 38 = \frac{5x+10}{5} \Rightarrow 190 = 5x + 10 \Rightarrow 180 = 5x \Rightarrow x = 36$

47) **Choice C is correct**

The area of the floor is: $6\ cm \times 24\ cm = 144\ cm^2$

The number of tiles needed $= 144 \div 8 = 18$

48) **Choice B is correct**

Use the average formula: average (mean) $= \frac{sum\ of\ terms}{number\ of\ terms} = \frac{9+12+15+16+19+16+14.5}{7} =$ 14.5

49) **Choice D is correct**

If each book weighs $\frac{1}{5}$ pound, then 1 pound = 5 books. To find the number of books in 50 pounds, simply multiply this 5 by 50: $50 \times 5 = 250$

50) **Choice C is correct**

The weight of 12.2 meters of this rope is: $12.2 \times 600\ g = 7{,}320\ g$

$1kg\ = 1{,}000g$, then, $7{,}320\ g \div 1{,}000 = 7.32\ kg$

51) **Choice C is correct**

4% of the volume of the solution is alcohol. Let x be the volume of the solution.

Then: $4\%\ of\ x = 24\ ml \Rightarrow 0.04\,x = 24 \Rightarrow x = 24 \div 0.04 = 600$

52) **Choice C is correct**

Use the volume of square pyramid formula.

$V = \frac{1}{3}a^2h \Rightarrow V = \frac{1}{3}\ (12\ m)^2 \times 10\ m \Rightarrow V = 480\ m^3$

53) **Choice B is correct**

$average\ = \frac{sum\ of\ terms}{number\ of\ terms}$

The sum of the weight of all girls is: $18 \times 60 = 1{,}080\ kg$

The sum of the weight of all boys is: $32 \times 62 = 1{,}984\ kg$

The sum of the weight of all students is: $1{,}080 + 1{,}984 = 3{,}064\ kg$

average $= \frac{3{,}064}{50} = 61.28$

54) **Choice C is correct**

Let x be the original price.

If the price of a laptop is decreased by 10% to $360, then:

90% of $x = 360 \Rightarrow 0.90x = 360 \Rightarrow x = 360 \div 0.90 = 400$

55) **Choice B is correct**

Write the numbers in order: $4, 5, 8, 9, 13, 15, 18$

Since there are 7 numbers (7 is odd), then the median is the number in the middle, which is 9.

56) **Choice D is correct**

Formula for the Surface area of a cylinder is:

$SA = 2\pi r^2 + 2\pi rh \rightarrow 150\pi = 2\pi r^2 + 2\pi r(10) \rightarrow r^2 + 10r - 75 = 0$

Factor the expression and solve:

$r^2 + 10r - 75 = 0 \rightarrow (r + 15)(r - 5) = 0 \rightarrow r = 5 \text{ or } r = -15 \ (unacceptable)$

57) **Choice A is correct**

Let x be the number of years. Therefore, \$2,000 per year equals $2{,}000x$.

Starting from \$24,000 annual salary means you should add that amount to $2{,}000x$.

Income more than that is: $I > 2{,}000x + 24{,}000$

SHSAT Mathematics Practice Test 2

1) **The answer is 64**

The area of the circle is 16π, then, its diameter is 8.
$Area\ of\ a\ circle = \pi r^2 = 16\pi \rightarrow r^2 = 16 \rightarrow r = 4$
Radius of the circle is 4 and diameter is twice of it, 8.
One side of the square equals to the diameter of the circle. Then:
Area of square $= side \times side = 8 \times 8 = 64$

2) **The answer is 9**

The median of a set of data is the value located in the middle of the data set.
Combine the two sets provided, and organize them in increasing order:

$$\{1, 3, 4, 6, 8, 10, 12, 14, 15, 17\}$$

Since there are 10 numbers (an even number of items) in the resulting list, the median is the average of the two middle numbers. Median $= \frac{(8+10)}{2} = 9$

3) **The answer is 2.25**

Write a proportion and solve for the missing number. $\frac{32}{12} = \frac{6}{x} \rightarrow 32x = 6 \times 12 = 72$

$$32x = 72 \rightarrow x = \frac{72}{32} = 2.25\ ft$$

4) **The answer is 42**

Plug in the value of x and y. $3(x - 2y) + (2 - x)^2$ When $x = 5$ and $y = -3$
$x = 5$ and $y = -3$
$3(x - 2y) + (2 - x)^2 = 3(5 - 2(-3)) + (2 - 5)^2 = 3(5 + 6) + (-3)^2 = 33 + 9 = 42$

5) **The answer is 175**

$-60 = 115 - x$, First, subtract 115 from both sides of the equation. Then:
$-60 - 115 = 115 - 115 - x \rightarrow -175 = -x$
Multiply both sides by (-1): $\rightarrow x = 175$

6) **Choice B is correct**

The area of the non-shaded region is equal to the area of the bigger rectangle subtracted by the area of smaller rectangle.
Area of the bigger rectangle $= 12 \times 16 = 192$
Area of the smaller rectangle $= 10 \times 4 = 40$
Area of the non-shaded region $= 192 - 40 = 152$

7) **Choice D is correct**

In the figure angle A is labeled $(3x - 2)$ and it measures 37. Thus, $3x - 2 = 37$ and $3x = 39$ or $x = 13$. That means that angle B, which is labeled $(5x)$, must measure $5 \times 13 = 65$.
Since the three angles of a triangle must add up to 180,
$37 + 65 + y - 8 = 180$, then: $y + 94 = 108 \rightarrow y = 180 - 94 = 86$

8) **Choice A is correct**

Simplify and combine like terms.
$(6x^3 - 8x^2 + 2x^4) - (4x^2 - 2x^4 + 2x^3) \Rightarrow (6x^3 - 8x^2 + 2x^4) - 4x^2 + 2x^4 - 2x^3$
$\Rightarrow 4x^4 + 4x^3 - 12x^2$

9) **Choice C is correct**

Let's find the mean (average), mode and median of the number of cities for each type of pollution. Number of cities for each type of pollution: $6, 3, 4, 9, 8$
$average\ (mean) = \frac{sum\ of\ terms}{number\ of\ terms} = \frac{6+3+4+9+8}{5} = \frac{30}{5} = 6$
The Median is the number in the middle. To find median, first list numbers in order from smallest to largest. $3, 4, 6, 8, 9$. The median of the data is 6.
Mode is the number which appears most often in a set of numbers. Therefore, there is no mode in the set of numbers. Median = Mean, then, $a = c$

10) **Choice A is correct**

Percent of cities in the type of pollution A: $\frac{6}{10} \times 100 = 60\%$
Percent of cities in the type of pollution C: $\frac{4}{10} \times 100 = 40\%$
Percent of cities in the type of pollution E: $\frac{9}{10} \times 100 = 90\%$

11)**Choice A is correct**

Let the number of cities should be added to type of pollutions B be x. Then:

$$\frac{x+3}{8} = 0.625 \rightarrow x+3 = 8 \times 0.625 \rightarrow x+3 = 5 \rightarrow x = 2$$

12)**Choice D is correct**

Let x be total number of cards in the box, then number of red cards is: $x - 246$

The probability of choosing a red card is one third. Then: $probability = \frac{1}{3} = \frac{x-132}{x}$

Use cross multiplication to solve for x.

$x \times 1 = 3(x - 246) \rightarrow x = 3x - 738 \rightarrow 2x = 738 \rightarrow x = 369$

13)**Choice B is correct**

Subtract $\frac{1}{6b}$ and $\frac{1}{b^2}$ from both sides of the equation. Then:

$\frac{1}{6b^2} + \frac{1}{6b} = \frac{1}{b^2} \rightarrow \frac{1}{6b^2} - \frac{1}{b^2} = -\frac{1}{6b}$

Multiply both numerator and denominator of the fraction $\frac{1}{b^2}$ by 6. Then:

$\frac{1}{6b^2} - \frac{6}{6b^2} = -\frac{1}{6b}$

Simplify the first side of the equation: $-\frac{5}{6b^2} = -\frac{1}{6b}$

Use cross multiplication method: $30b = 6b^2 \rightarrow 30 = 6b \rightarrow b = 5$

14)**Choice C is correct**

The population is increased by 15% and 20%. 15% increase changes the population to 115% of original population. For the second increase, multiply the result by 120%.

$(1.15) \times (1.20) = 1.38 = 138\%$. 38 percent of the population is increased after two years.

15)**Choice D is correct**

Solve for x. $-2 \leq 2x - 4 < 8 \Rightarrow$ (add 4 all sides) $-2 + 4 \leq 2x - 4 + 4 < 8 + 4 \Rightarrow$ $2 \leq 2x < 12 \Rightarrow$ (divide all sides by 2) $1 \leq x < 6$

x is between 1 and 6. Choice D represent this inequality.

16) **Choice D is correct**

Use Volume of a box formula: $length \times width \times height = 4 \times 5 \times 6 = 120$

17) **Choice C is correct**

y is the intersection of the three circles. Therefore, it must be odd (from circle A), negative (from circle B), and multiple of 5 (from circle C).
From the choices provided, only -5 is odd, negative and multiple of 5.

18) **Choice B is correct**

Recall that the formula for the average is: $Average = \frac{sum\ of\ data}{number\ of\ data}$
First, compute the total weight of all balls in the basket: $25\ g = \frac{total\ weight}{20\ balls}$
$25\ g \times 20 =$ total weight $= 500\ g$. Next, find the total weight of the 5 largest marbles:
$40\ g = \frac{total\ weight}{5\ marbles} \rightarrow 40\ g \times 5 =$ total weight $= 200\ g$
The total weight of the heaviest balls is $200\ g$. Then, the total weight of the remaining 15 balls is $300\ g$. $500\ g - 200\ g = 300\ g$.
The average weight of the remaining balls: Average $= \frac{300\ g}{15\ marbles} = 20\ g$ per ball

19) **Choice C is correct**

To find the number of possible outfit combinations, multiply number of options for each factor: $3 \times 5 \times 4 = 60$

20) **Choice A is correct**

In the stadium the ratio of home fans to visiting fans in a crowd is $5:7$. Therefore, total number of fans must be divisible by $12: 5 + 7 = 12$.
Let's review the choices:
A. $12{,}324 \rightarrow 12{,}324 \div 12 = 1{,}027$
B. $42{,}326 \rightarrow 42{,}326 \div 12 = 3{,}527.166$
C. $44{,}566 \rightarrow 44{,}566 \div 12 = 3{,}713.833$
D. $66{,}812 \rightarrow 66{,}812 \div 12 = 5{,}567.666$
Only choice A when divided by 12 results a whole number.

21) **Choice C is correct**

Three times of 24,000 is 72,000. One sixth of them cancelled their tickets. One sixth of 72,000 equals 12,000($\frac{1}{6} \times 72{,}000 = 12{,}000$).

60,000($72{,}000 - 12{,}000 = 60{,}000$) fans are attending this week.

22) **Choice A is correct**

The area of the square is 595.36. Therefore, the side of the square is square root of the area.

$\sqrt{595.36} = 24.4$

Four times the side of the square is the perimeter: $4 \times 24.4 = 97.6$

23) **Choice D is correct**

Fist convert mixed numbers to fractions: $2\frac{2}{3} - 1\frac{5}{6} = 2\frac{4}{6} - 1\frac{5}{6} = \frac{16}{6} - \frac{11}{6} = \frac{5}{6}$

24) **Choice A is correct**

The width of the rectangle is twice its length. Let x be the length. Then, width $= 2x$

Perimeter of the rectangle is 2 (width + length) $= 2(2x + x) = 60 \Rightarrow 6x = 60 \Rightarrow x = 10$

Length of the rectangle is 10 meters.

25) **Choice D is correct**

Change the numbers to decimal and then compare.

$\frac{2}{3} = 0.666\ldots$

0.68

$67\% = 0.67$

$\frac{4}{5} = 0.80$

Then: $\frac{2}{3} < 67\% < 0.68 < \frac{4}{5}$

26) **Choice C is correct**

$$average\ (mean) = \frac{sum\ of\ terms}{number\ of\ terms} \Rightarrow 88 = \frac{sum\ of\ terms}{50} \Rightarrow sum = 88 \times 50 = 4{,}400$$

The difference of 94 and 69 is 25. Therefore, 25 should be subtracted from the sum.

$4{,}400 - 25 = 4{,}375$

$mean = \frac{sum\ of\ terms}{number\ of\ terms} \Rightarrow mean = \frac{4{,}375}{50} = 87.5$

27) **Choice D is correct**

Let x be the number of current stamps in the collection. Then:

$\frac{6}{5}x - x = 100 \rightarrow \frac{1}{5}x = 100 \rightarrow x = 500$

50% more of 500 is: $500 + 0.50 \times 500 = 500 + 250 = 750$.

28) **Choice B is correct**

To get a sum of 6 for two dice, we can get 5 different options: $(5,1), (4,2), (3,3), (2,4), (1,5)$

To get a sum of 9 for two dice, we can get 4 different options: $(6,3), (5,4), (4,5), (3,6)$

Therefore, there are 9 options to get the sum of 6 or 9.

Since, we have $6 \times 6 = 36$ total options, the probability of getting a sum of 6 and 9 is 9 out of 36 or $\frac{1}{4}$.

29) **Choice D is correct**

Use formula of rectangle prism volume.

$V = (length)(width)(height) \Rightarrow 2{,}000 = (25)(10)(height) \Rightarrow height = 2{,}000 \div 250 = 8$

30) **Choice B is correct**

The diagonal of the square is 8. Let x be the side.

Use Pythagorean Theorem: $a^2 + b^2 = c^2$

$x^2 + x^2 = 8^2 \Rightarrow 2x^2 = 8^2 \Rightarrow 2x^2 = 64 \Rightarrow x^2 = 32 \Rightarrow x = \sqrt{32}$

The area of the square is: $\sqrt{32} \times \sqrt{32} = 32$

31) **Choice B is correct**

The sum of 8 numbers is greater than 240 and less than 320. Then, the average of the 8 numbers must be greater than 30 and less than 40.

$\frac{240}{8} < x < \frac{320}{8} \rightarrow 30 < x < 40$

The only choice that is between 30 and 40 is 35.

32) **Choice B is correct**

Probability $= \frac{\textit{number of desired outcomes}}{\text{number of total outcomes}} = \frac{18}{12+18+18+24} = \frac{18}{72} = \frac{1}{4}$

33) **Choice D is correct**

Use the average formula: average $= \frac{\textit{sum of terms}}{\textit{number of terms}} \Rightarrow$ (average of 6 numbers)

$12 = \frac{\textit{sum of numbers}}{6} \Rightarrow$ sum of 6 numbers is $12 \times 6 = 72$

(Average of 4 numbers) $10 = \frac{\textit{sum of numbers}}{4} \Rightarrow$sum of 4 numbers is $10 \times 4 = 40$

Sum of 6 numbers – sum of 4 numbers = sum of 2 numbers $72 - 40 = 32$

Average of 2 numbers $= \frac{32}{2} = 16$

34) **Choice B is correct**

The angles on a straight line add up to 180 degrees. Then: $x + 25 + y + 2x + y = 180$

Then, $3x + 2y = 180 - 25 \rightarrow 3(35) + 2y = 155 \rightarrow 2y = 155 - 105 = 50 \rightarrow y = 25$

35) **Choice B is correct**

The perimeter of the trapezoid is 38 cm. Therefore, the missing side is:

$38 - 13 - 9 - 4 = 12$. Area of a trapezoid: $A = \frac{1}{2}h(b_1 + b_2) = \frac{1}{2}(12)(4 + 9) = 78$

36) **Choice A is correct**

First, find the number. Let x be the number. Write the equation and solve for x.

150% of a number is 75, then: $1.5 \times x = 75 \Rightarrow x = 75 \div 1.5 = 50$

90% of 50 is: $0.9 \times 50 = 45$

37) **Choice B is correct**

If two triangles are similar, then the ratios of corresponding sides are equal.

$\frac{AC}{AE} = \frac{BC}{DE} = \frac{18}{9} = 2, \frac{AC}{AE} = 2$

This ratio can be used to find the length of AC: $AC = 2 \times AE$, $AC = 2 \times 9 \rightarrow AC = 18$

The length of AE is given as 9 and we now know the length of AC is 18, therefore:

$EC = AC - AE$ $\qquad EC = 18 - 9,$ $\qquad EC = 9$

38) **Choice A is correct**

Let x be the number of new shoes the team can purchase. Therefore, the team can purchase $120x$. The team had \$20,000 and spent \$14,000. Now the team can spend on new shoes \$6,000 at most. Now, write the inequality: $120x + 14{,}000 \leq 20{,}000$

39) **Choice B is correct**

The probability of choosing a Hearts is $\frac{13}{52} = \frac{1}{4}$

40) **Choice D is correct**

First, find the sum of five numbers.

Average $= \frac{sum\ of\ terms}{number\ of\ terms} \Rightarrow 24 = \frac{sum\ of\ 5\ numbers}{5} \Rightarrow$ sum of 5 numbers $= 24 \times 5 = 120$

The sum of 5 numbers is 120. If a sixth number that is greater than 42 is added to these numbers, then the sum of 6 numbers must be greater than 162.

$120 + 42 = 162$

If the number was 42, then the average of the numbers is:

Average $= \frac{sum\ of\ terms}{number\ of\ terms} = \frac{162}{6} = 27$

Since the number is bigger than 42. Then, the average of six numbers must be greater than 27. Choice D is greater than 27.

41) **Choice D is correct**

Let E age of Ella, we know Ella is 4 years older than Ava: $E = 4 + A \rightarrow A = S - 3$

42) **Choice B is correct**

Let L be the length of the rectangular and W be the width of the rectangular. Then,

$$L = 4W + 3$$

The perimeter of the rectangle is 36 meters. Therefore: $2L + 2W = 36$,

$$L + W = 18$$

Replace the value of L from the first equation into the second equation and solve for W:

$$(4W + 3) + W = 18 \rightarrow 5W + 3 = 18 \rightarrow 5W = 15 \rightarrow W = 3$$

The width of the rectangle is 3 meters and its length is: $L = 4W + 3 = 4(3) + 3 = 15$

The area of the rectangle is: $Length \times Width = 3 \times 15 = 45$

43) **Choice C is correct**

The ratio of boy to girls is 4:7. Therefore, there are 4 boys out of 11 students. To find the answer, first divide the total number of students by 11, then multiply the result by 4.

$44 \div 11 = 4 \Rightarrow 4 \times 4 = 16$

There are 16 boys and 28 (44 – 16) girls. So, 12 more boys should be enrolled to make the ratio 1:1

44) **Choice A is correct**

2,500 out of 55,000 equals to $\frac{2,500}{55,000} = \frac{25}{550} = \frac{1}{22}$

45) **Choice D is correct**

Jason needs an 75% average to pass for five exams. Therefore, the sum of 5 exams must be at lease $5 \times 75 = 375$. The sum of 4 exams is: $68 + 72 + 85 + 90 = 315$

The minimum score Jason can earn on his fifth and final test to pass is: $375 - 315 = 60$

46) **Choice D is correct**

Isolate and solve for x. $\frac{2}{3}x + \frac{1}{6} = \frac{1}{3} \Rightarrow \frac{2}{3}x = \frac{1}{3} - \frac{1}{6} = \frac{1}{6} \Rightarrow \frac{2}{3}x = \frac{1}{6}$

Multiply both sides by the reciprocal of the coefficient of x. $(\frac{3}{2})\frac{2}{3}x = \frac{1}{6}(\frac{3}{2}) \Rightarrow$
$x = \frac{3}{12} = \frac{1}{4}$

47) **Choice C is correct**

Surface Area of a Cylinder $= 2\pi r\ (r + h)$, The radius of the cylinder is 3 $(6 \div 2)$ inches and its height is 8 inches. Therefore, Surface Area of a cylinder $= 2\pi(3)(3 + 8) = 66\ \pi$

48) **Choice C is correct**

The square of a number is $\frac{25}{64}$, then the number is the square root of $\frac{25}{64}$ â
$\sqrt{\frac{25}{64}} = \frac{5}{8}$
The cube of the number is: $(\frac{5}{8})^3 = \frac{125}{512}$

49) **Choice B is correct**

Write the numbers in order: $2, 19, 27, 28, 35, 44, 67$
Median is the number in the middle. So, the median is 28.

50) **Choice D is correct**

Use Pythagorean Theorem: $a^2 + b^2 = c^2$
$6^2 + 8^2 = c^2 \Rightarrow 100 = c^2 \Rightarrow \text{c} = 10$

51) **Choice B is correct**

Plug in 104 for F and then solve for C.
$\text{C} = \frac{5}{9}(\text{F} - 32) \rightarrow \text{C} = \frac{5}{9}(104 - 32) \rightarrow \text{C} = \frac{5}{9}(72) = 40$

52) **Choice C is correct**

Let x be the number. Write the equation and solve for x.
$40\%\ of\ x = 4 \rightarrow 0.40\ x = 4 x = 4\ \div 0.40 = 10$

53) **Choice D is correct**

Let x be all expenses, then $\frac{22}{100}x = \$660 \rightarrow x = \frac{100 \times \$660}{22} = \$3{,}000$
He spent for his rent: $\frac{27}{100} \times \$3{,}000 = \$810$

54) **Choice C is correct**

The distance between Jason and Joe is 9 miles. Jason running at 5.5 miles per hour and Joe is running at the speed of 7 miles per hour. Therefore, every hour the distance is 1.5 miles less. $9 \div 1.5 = 6$

55) **Choice D is correct**

The failing rate is 11 out of $55 = \frac{11}{55}$. Change the fraction to percent: $\frac{11}{55} \times 100\% = 20\%$

20 Percent of students failed. Therefore, 80 percent of students passed the exam.

56) **Choice B is correct**

Use simple interest formula: $I = prt$

(I = interest, p = principal, r = rate, t = time) $\rightarrow I = (12{,}000)(0.035)(2) = 840$

57) **Choice B is correct.**

To find the area of the shaded region subtract the area of the smaller circle from bigger circle.

$S_{bigger} - S_{smaller} = \pi (r_{bigger})^2 - \pi (r_{smaller})^2 \Rightarrow S_{bigger} - S_{smaller} =$

$$\pi(6)^2 - \pi (4)^2 \Rightarrow 36\pi - 16\pi = 20\pi$$

Effortless Math's SHSAT Online Center

... So Much More Online!

Effortless Math Online SHSAT Math Center offers a complete study program, including the following:

- ✓ Step-by-step instructions on how to prepare for the SHSAT Math test
- ✓ Numerous SHSAT Math worksheets to help you measure your math skills
- ✓ Complete list of SHSAT Math formulas
- ✓ Video lessons for SHSAT Math topics
- ✓ Full-length SHSAT Math practice tests
- ✓ And much more...

No Registration Required.

Visit **EffortlessMath.com/SHSAT** to find your online SHSAT Math resources.

Receive the PDF version of this book or get another FREE book!

Author's Final Note

I hope you enjoyed reading this book. You've made it through the book! Great job!

First of all, thank you for purchasing this study guide. I know you could have picked any number of books to help you prepare for your SHSAT Math test, but you picked this book and for that I am extremely grateful.

It took me years to write this study guide for the SHSAT Math because I wanted to prepare a comprehensive SHSAT Math study guide to help test takers make the most effective use of their valuable time while preparing for the test.

After teaching and tutoring math courses for over a decade, I've gathered my personal notes and lessons to develop this study guide. It is my greatest hope that the lessons in this book could help you prepare for your test successfully.

If you have any questions, please contact me at reza@effortlessmath.com and I will be glad to assist. Your feedback will help me to greatly improve the quality of my books in the future and make this book even better. Furthermore, I expect that I have made a few minor errors somewhere in this study guide. If you think this to be the case, please let me know so I can fix the issue as soon as possible.

If you enjoyed this book and found some benefit in reading this, I'd like to hear from you and hope that you could take a quick minute to post a review on the book's Amazon page. To leave your valuable feedback, please visit: amzn.to/30WOStK

Or scan this QR code.

I personally go over every single review, to make sure my books really are reaching out and helping students and test takers. Please help me help SHSAT Math test takers, by leaving a review!

I wish you all the best in your future success!

Reza Nazari

Math teacher and author